MASTERPIECES

FROM THE NATIONAL GALLERY

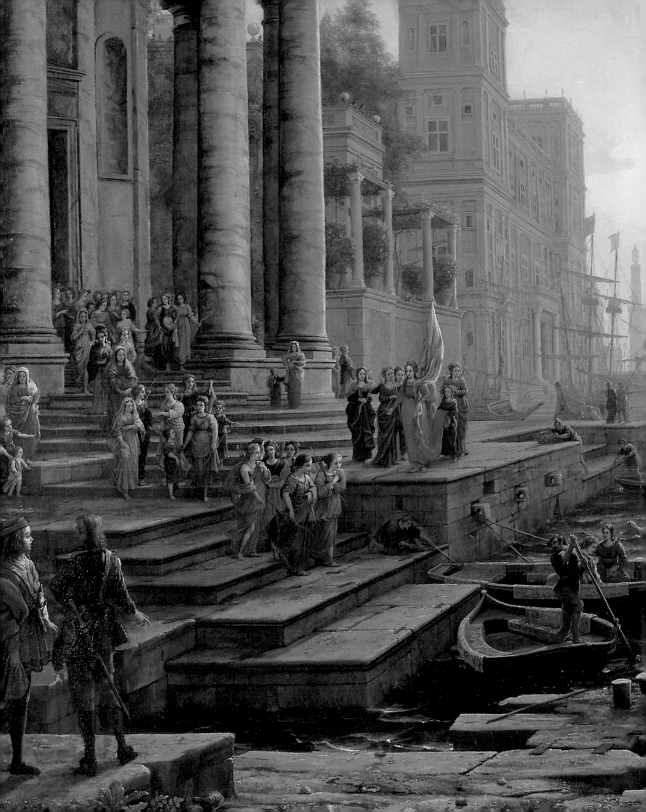

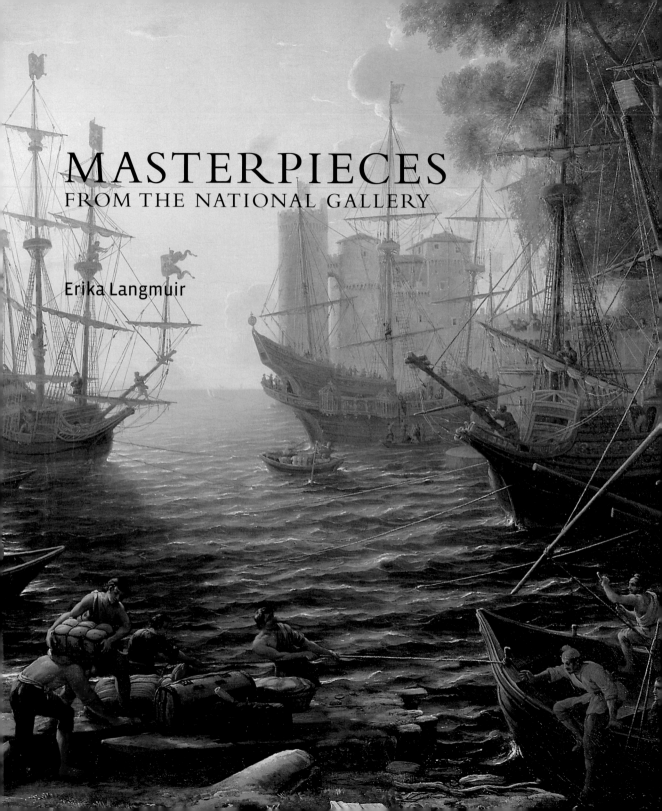

MASTERPIECES

FROM THE NATIONAL GALLERY

Erika Langmuir

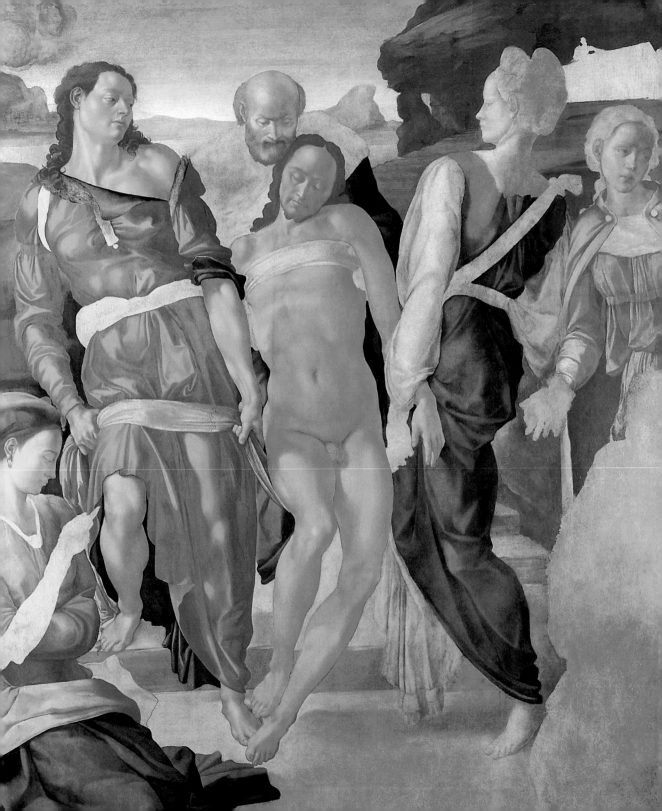

CONTENTS

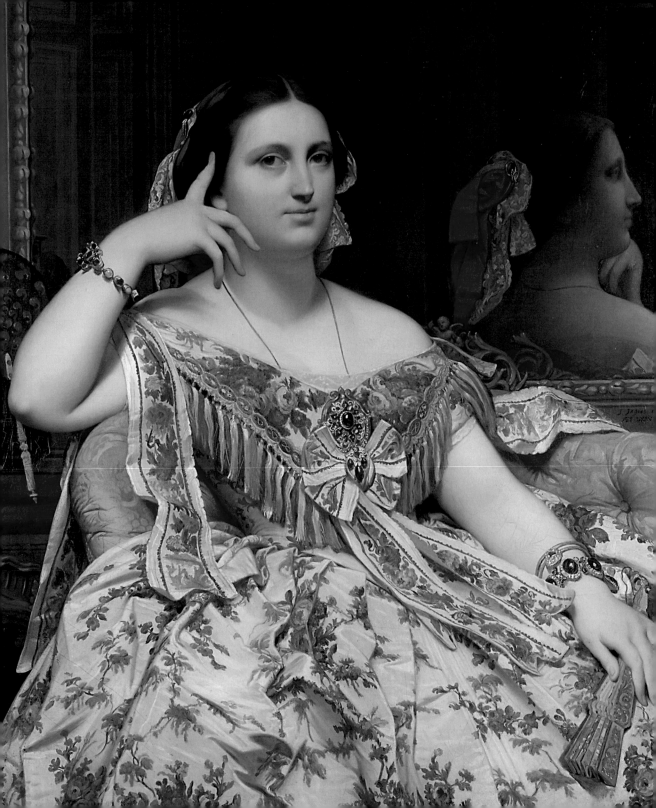

DIRECTOR'S FOREWORD

Every visitor to the National Gallery could benefit from having a friendly and knowledgeable guide to the paintings: to draw attention to particular techniques and styles, to explain how they came to be painted and tell the stories behind them. In this way, the experience of visiting the gallery is enriched by what you know about the origins of the works. Reading about the paintings encourages you to look at them afresh, with a greater sense of their meaning and the skills to interpret them.

Masterpieces provides this very information. It can be read either before a visit in preparation, while you are wandering through the galleries or, once you have returned home, as a reminder of what you have seen. The guide concentrates on the great masterpieces of the collection – from the *Wilton Diptych* painted in the late fourteenth century, to Van Gogh's *Sunflowers* painted at the end of the nineteenth century – giving a good idea of the amazing wealth of the National Gallery's collection.

I hope you will enjoy your visit to the National Gallery. It is somewhere to come not just to see best-loved masterpieces, but to experience a collection of extraordinary range – major works alongside lesser known, British alongside French, German and Italian, works from the early Renaissance to late Impressionism. It is a place to come back to time and again to discover more about the grand traditions of western European painting – the traditions which have helped shape the visual expression and experience of our own time.

CHARLES SAUMAREZ SMITH
Director
The National Gallery, London

FROM GIOTTO TO DÜRER
Paintings 1250–1500

Opened in July 1991, the Sainsbury Wing, with its dark grey stone arches and pale plaster walls recalling the cool interiors of Florentine Renaissance churches, was designed to house the earliest paintings in the Gallery (fig.1).

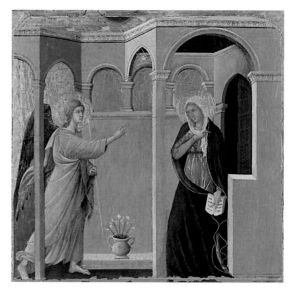

Fig.1 **Duccio** *The Annunciation*, 1311

The setting is appropriate, since most of these works – including some of the greatest, like Piero della Francesca's *Baptism of Christ*, Bermejo's *Saint Michael triumphant over the Devil with the Donor Antonio Juan* and Leonardo da Vinci's *'Virgin of the Rocks'* – were originally made for churches, though not only Italian ones. Set above the altar table, such pictures showed the holy personage to whom the church, or a particular chapel, was dedicated, and formed a backdrop to religious services conducted at the altar. Smaller, portable altarpieces were intended for the eyes of a single worshipper: *The Wilton Diptych*, depicting King Richard II of England in prayer before Christ and the Virgin Mary, was

almost certainly painted for the King's own devotions. Other small pictures on Christian themes were made for the home (fig.2), as aids to pious meditation rather than to formal worship. In this period, piety and aesthetic pleasure were not as firmly differentiated as they are now, and the original owner of Dürer's *Saint Jerome* could both enjoy the painting as pure landscape, and draw religious inspiration from the figure of the penitent saint.

8

But not all the paintings in the Sainsbury Wing were inspired by religion. Many simply record people's features and social status. Jan van Eyck's *'Arnolfini Portrait'*, while not depicting an actual wedding, confirms the prosperous wedded state of an Italian merchant and his wife resident in the Netherlands. Bellini's *Doge Leonardo Loredan* was painted to celebrate this elderly nobleman's election as ceremonial head of the Most Serene Republic of Venice. Other secular pictures, that now appear as independent works of art, were originally part of the costly decoration of a room or a piece of furniture. Some – like Botticelli's *Mars and Venus* – depict characters or stories from ancient mythology; others refer to an event in history.

With the exception of murals, most surviving pictures from this period were painted on wooden panels. Italian artists worked above all in tempera – pigments suspended in quick-drying egg yolk or whole egg. The preferred medium in northern Europe was slow-drying oil paint, which made possible a more realistic depiction of light and shade and varied textures. Both oils and tempera were brushed on over a smooth, white, chalk or gesso ground, and both required meticulous pre-planning. Artists both north and south of the Alps also often used gold leaf, which was beaten out

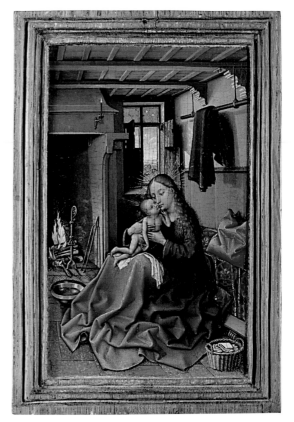

Fig.2 **Workshop of Campin (Jaques Daret?)** *The Virgin and Child in an Interior*, 1435

thinly from gold coins and applied either as background to the coloured areas or as luminous lines on the painted surface. The gold was often incised or punched to reflect light, or in imitation of gold cloth. To recapture something of their original effect, we must imagine the gilded altarpieces of the Sainsbury Wing as glittering in the flickering light of church candles.

1. **The Wilton Diptych** (about 1395–9)

Egg on oak   each wing 53 × 37 cm

All gold and precious blue lapis lazuli, this is one of the most exquisite paintings surviving from the Middle Ages, and it embodies all the religious and courtly ideals of medieval Europe. Richard II of England has dedicated his kingdom, in the form of a globe atop the banner of Christ's Resurrection, to the Virgin Mary, Queen of Heaven. The Christ Child, having accepted it on her behalf, now blesses Richard as her viceroy. Kneeling on the bare ground before a vision of the flower-strewn Garden of Paradise, the king is presented to the celestial assembly by his patron saint, John the Baptist, and two saintly predecessors, Kings Edmund and Edward the Confessor. Born on 6 January, when the Church celebrates both Epiphany – the three kings' Adoration of the new-born Christ – and Christ's Baptism in the River Jordan, Richard himself probably commissioned this altarpiece for his own devotions, proclaiming simultaneously his hope of Salvation and belief in his God-given right to rule.

• A diptych is a picture in two panels hinged to open like a book. Closed, it could be transported without damaging the inside; open, it could stand on a shelf or altar and serve as an aid to prayer. Marriage portraits were sometimes painted as non-religious diptychs.

• All the gold surfaces here are made of gold leaf, finely punched to catch the light. The design of the Christ Child's halo shows the crown of thorns that will later be forced onto his head, and the nails with which he will be crucified. The artist has portrayed a Child born to suffer and die in atonement for humanity's sins.

• The orb or globe on top of Christ's banner contains the tiny image of a green island, crowned with a white castle and set in a silver-leaf sea, now tarnished. This is like the 'patterne of England' offered by Richard II for the Virgin Mary's dowry, recorded on a lost altarpiece.

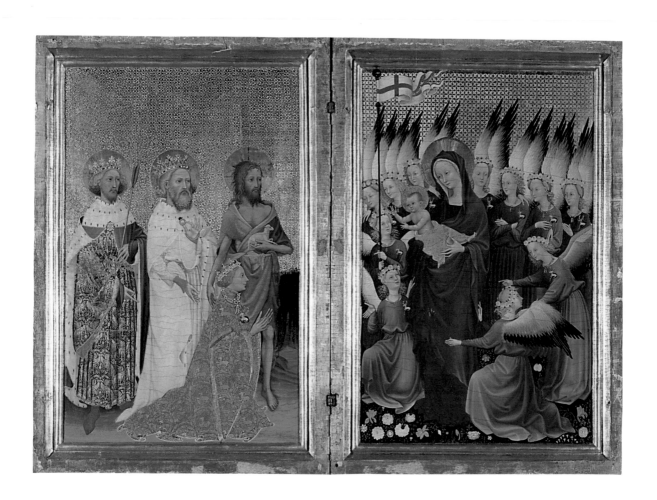

2. Portrait of Giovanni(?) Arnolfini and his Wife (1434)

Oil on oak 82.2 × 60 cm

The inscription on the back wall, translated as 'Jan van Eyck was here/1434', does not mean, as is often asserted, that this famous marriage portrait records an actual wedding ceremony. The Netherlandish painter has placed his friends – an expatriate Italian merchant and his wife – in an imaginary room, emblematic of their married state. He 'was here' because *only* he was here in this made-up room. Through patient observation of the effects of light on differently textured and shaped surfaces, and exceedingly skilful manipulation of slow-drying oil paints, van Eyck created the illusion of a real interior, seemingly lit through the window in the picture and a second lightsource in the viewer's own space – possibly the door reflected in the convex mirror. The human inhabitants of this room seem less real than the vibrant living light that defines the space and everything in it: prayer beads, a brass chandelier, a mirror, muddy wooden pattens, the pockmarked skins of oranges, a silky haired little dog, wood, velvet, wool, linen, fur. Van Eyck did not, as it is sometimes said, invent oil paints, but he pioneered the optical realism they made possible, and his art opens our eyes to the actual world around us. What is the colour, for example, of polished brass? Not, the viewer learns here, a single 'brass yellow', but an unexpectedly wide range of tones from almost white through bright gold to nearly black.

VAN EYCK IN
THE NATIONAL GALLERY
Other paintings by van Eyck are *Portrait of a Man* (*Léal Souvenir*), 1432, and *Portrait of a Man* (*Self Portrait?*), 1433. A fourth picture, *Marco Barbarigo*, about 1449, is thought to have been painted in London by a close follower.

• The expensive hand-blown mirror on the back wall is not here just to demonstrate the Arnolfini's wealth. The little paintings under glass set in its frame show scenes from Christ's Passion, leading up to his Crucifixion and Resurrection: this mirror is like the eye of God, in which our earthly behaviour is reflected in the light of eternity.

• Not all the dark areas around Giovanni Arnolfini's shoes are shadows. Since oil paint becomes translucent with age, we can now see where van Eyck changed his mind about how to position Arnolfini's feet. Such changes of mind directly on the panel or canvas are called *pentimenti*, 'repentances', and they only occur in oil painting.

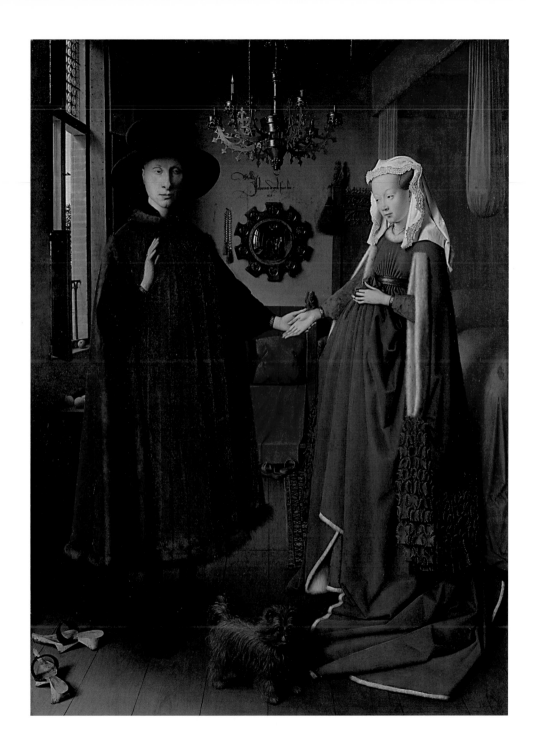

3. **The Baptism of Christ** (1450s)

Egg on poplar 167 × 116 cm

The world holds its breath in this painting; as hushed and still, ordered, cool and clear as a crystal. This is the moment when Christ, being baptised by Saint John in the River Jordan, is revealed as the Son of God. The Holy Spirit descends on him 'like a dove' (Mark 1:10) and his hands are closed in prayer to his Heavenly Father. It is a unique moment in history, and is also timeless. The original viewers would once have recognised Christ's divinity anew every time they worshipped beneath this altarpiece. Now in the National Gallery many still do, but for others today this lonely, pale figure at the centre of things is just a human being like ourselves. Stripped bare, he looks deeply into his own heart, reflecting on his destiny. We have all known decisive moments like this, when nothing will ever be the same again, and we ourselves will be changed. Soon the dove must fold its wings, the river flow again and the baptismal water will trickle down over Christ's head; and he will step forward to confront and embrace his future. Another man behind Christ readies himself for baptism. Because this picture shows a universal experience, Piero della Francesca has relocated Palestine to the familiar countryside of Tuscany, near his native town of Borgo San Sepolcro.

• Piero della Francesca used geometry to achieve this composition. The dove's outstretched wings mark the upper edge of a perfect square. The panel is divided in half vertically by an implicit line running from the middle of the arched top down through Christ's weight-bearing right foot.

• The white dove of the Holy Spirit also demonstrates Piero's study of the new Renaissance science of perspective. We see it perfectly foreshortened, as if it were flying at eye level straight at us.

• Borgo San Sepolcro (the modern Sansepolcro) was named 'Town of the Holy Sepulchre' because it was supposedly founded by pilgrims from the Holy Land, who brought back relics believed to come from the tomb where Christ was buried.

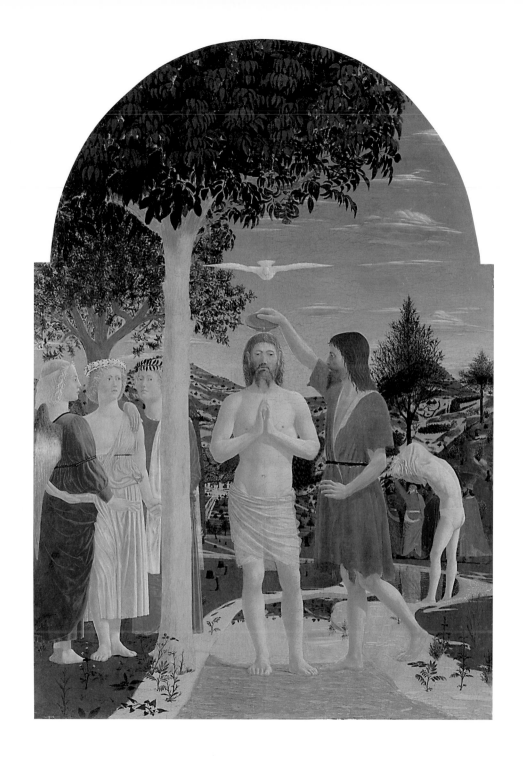

4. Saint Michael triumphant over the Devil with the Donor Antonio Juan (about 1468)

Oil and gold on wood   179 × 81.4 cm

The Archangel Michael is believed to be the Commander-in-Chief of God's armies, who expelled from Heaven the rebellious angels led by Satan. He was particularly venerated in Spain, because he was associated there with the Christian reconquest of Spanish territories long held by Muslims. Dressed in contemporary gilded armour, a gold-brocade priestly vestment and carrying a magnificent crystal-domed shield, Michael is shown here in the very act of slaying the devil. But traditionally he also has the task of weighing souls at the Last Judgment, to assess whether their virtues outweigh their sins. It is therefore both as a champion of Spain and as a judge of individual souls that he is venerated here by Antonio Juan, a knight and the feudal lord of the town of Tous, near Valencia, for whose church of San Miguel this altarpiece was painted – at Juan's expense. Bermejo's accomplished use of oil paints, responsible for both the intense realism and the decorative splendour of this picture, demonstrates the influence of Netherlandish art (see van Eyck) on Spanish painters.

• Michael's armour appears to be made of gold, not steel, and is set with jewels. The polished breastplate shows reflections of the Gothic spires and towers of a great city, which can only be the Heavenly Jerusalem – although the devil on whom Michael treads has already fallen down to earth.

• The devil appears as the beautiful Archangel's opposite. While Michael is impassive in victory, Satan – part reptile, bird, moth, bat, shell and hedgehog – squirms and screams like an unruly child. He is probably meant to represent all seven deadly sins: pride, wrath, envy, lust, gluttony, avarice and sloth.

• Juan's book shows verses from Psalms 51, 'Have mercy upon me, O God…' and 130, 'Out of the depths have I cried unto thee, O Lord'.

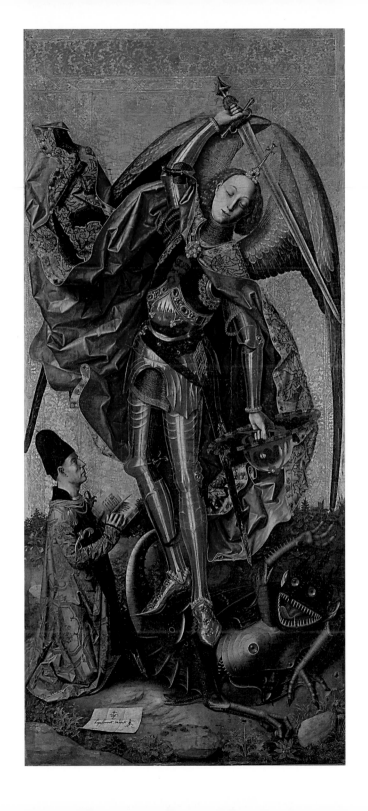

5. ## **Venus and Mars** (about 1485)

Egg and oil on poplar   painted surface 69.2 × 173.4 cm

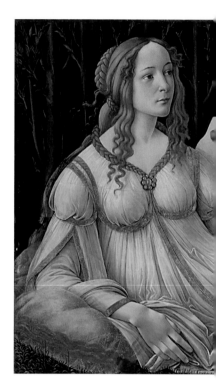

This picture is one of a small number of mythological paintings for which Botticelli is now famous. It was almost certainly made to decorate the backboard of a bench or chest in the chamber of a Florentine town house, newly furnished for a wedding. Lying on cushions on the grass in front of a copse of evergreen laurel Venus, goddess of love and beauty, watches while her lover Mars, god of war, sleeps. Not even the conch shell blown in his ear by mischievous baby satyrs – half-child, half-goat – can wake him, nor can the wasps buzzing nearby. While the characters are drawn from classical mythology, Venus' hair-style, jewellery and translucent gown – and Mars' armour – owe more to contemporary fashion than to ancient art. Both the obviously intended humorous interpretation of the scene – 'lovemaking exhausts men, but invigorates women' – and its serious underlying message – 'love conquers all' – would have been thought appropriate sentiments in marriage celebrations. Botticelli, mainly a painter of religious subjects and portraits, was a friend of some of the leading Florentine poets and intellectuals of his day, and this picture, like the artist's celebrated *Primavera*, may have been influenced by a literary source, ancient or modern.

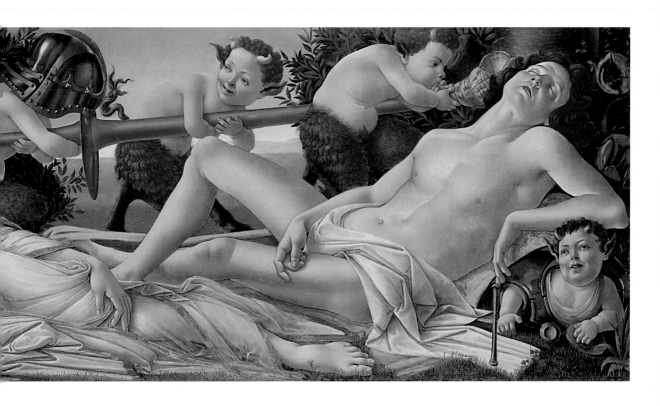

• Botticelli or botticello means 'little barrel'; the artist's real name was Alessandro Filipepi. He was the son of a Florentine tanner, but was brought up by his elder brother, a beater of gold leaf, who seems to have been the first to bear the nickname.

• The baby satyr with a helmet may have been inspired by the ancient Greek poet Lucian's description of a painting depicting the wedding of Alexander and Roxane, in which cupids play with Alexander's weapons and armour. Satyrs, even more than cupids, symbolise uninhibited sexual activity: Mars has been truly 'disarmed', and is too exhausted to make either love or war.

• Wasps are *vespe* in Italian, and were a punning emblem of the Vespucci family, for whom Botticelli is known to have worked. It has been suggested that this painting was made for them, but as there is no record of this, the insects' presence here may simply refer to the 'stings' of love.

6. The Doge Leonardo Loredan (1501–4)

Oil on poplar 61.6 × 45.1 cm

This evocative portrait was probably painted soon after the election in 1501 of Leonardo Loredan (1436–1521) as Doge, that is, head of state of the Venetian Republic. He is shown wearing the white ceremonial dress of horned cap and cape (in the luxurious material of damask), woven with gold thread adorned with bell-like buttons. Partly inspired by the sculpted portrait busts of ancient Rome, partly by Netherlandish painted portraits, the picture is a static official image. The Doge is set back from the viewer, behind a stone parapet on which a fictitious piece of paper or parchment – like a label attached to a specimen or a relic – bears the artist's signature. Yet there are intimations here of personality – even a meditation on old age, or perhaps faith. By graduating the blue behind the Doge, more intense at the top and lighter at the bottom of the picture, Bellini has transformed a conventional flat background into a sky, and the strongly directional light, reflecting in Loredan's eyes, suggests that he is looking towards the sun. Although to judge by its colour it is not yet setting, the sun must be fairly low – and this hint of passing time, combined with Loredan's aged face, recalls the old comparison between the duration of a day and the span of a human life. Night must fall. Yet Bellini, a devout Christian, often represents Salvation as the light of a new dawn – and perhaps that is also the hope he offers Doge Loredan in what is otherwise an entirely secular painting.

BELLINI IN
THE NATIONAL GALLERY
There are fourteen paintings in addition to this picture by the artist and his workshop in the Collection; among the most famous are the *Blood of the Redeemer*, probably 1460–5; *The Agony in the Garden*, about 1465, and *The Madonna of the Meadow*, about 1500.

• This portrait is less static than it seems. Although the catchlights (reflections) in both eyes are equally prominent, the right side of Loredan's face (on our left) is more strongly lit and severe – while the left side, in shadow, appears more benevolent.

• Hand-ground oil paints vary in density, and depending on the colour can be applied as thin transparent layers or thick opaque dabs and dashes. Bellini has exploited the pasty consistency of white and yellow pigments ground in oil, deliberately roughing the thick paint to simulate the gold and white weave of the damask.

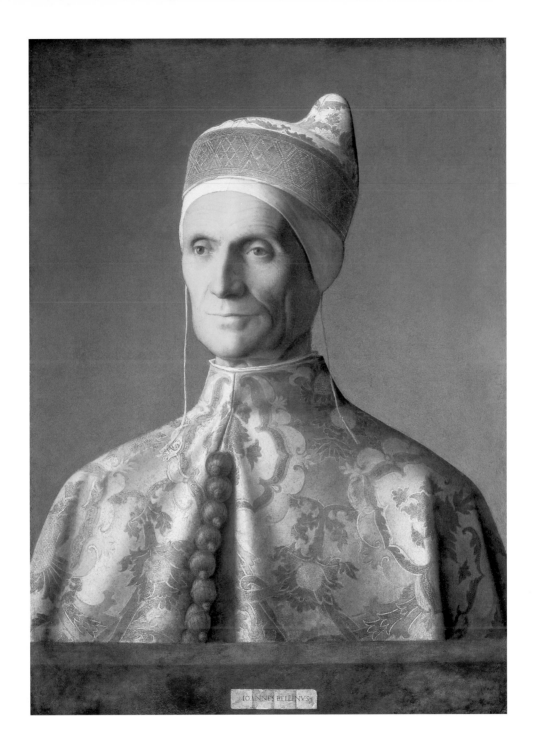

7. 'The Virgin of the Rocks' (about 1508)

Oil on wood   189.5 × 120 cm

This mysterious picture was painted as the central panel of an altarpiece for a lay brotherhood in Milan dedicated to the Immaculate Conception. Leonardo may have planned the composition before he received the commission on his arrival in the city in 1483, since it is a variation on a theme that had already preoccupied him in Florence, rather than a conventional image of the Immaculate Conception. Officially adopted as dogma by the Roman Catholic Church only in 1854, this doctrine concerns not the miraculous birth of Jesus but the Virgin Mary's exemption from Original Sin; it was normally represented by picturing her without the Christ Child. 'The Virgin of the Rocks' shows Mary not only with the Infant Christ, attended by an angel, but also sheltering the infant Saint John the Baptist under her cloak. The artist's patrons must have been puzzled, and worried about confusing the two infants, since John's traditional attribute, a reed cross, was added later, clumsily planted in one of Leonardo's exquisite studies of flowers. The figures, never fully finished, emerge from the shadows as from a dark cavern – an illusion originally enhanced by an elaborately carved frame. They could almost personify the forces of nature represented in the setting – as if their rite of reverence and regeneration mirrored primordial processes governing the ebb and flow of water, or the formation of rocks and fossils; the figures symbolise the flowering, death and rebirth of living organisms that are the true objects of Leonardo's veneration.

LEONARDO DA VINCI IN THE NATIONAL GALLERY

Leonardo's large drawing of *The Virgin and Child with Saint Anne and Saint John the Baptist*, perhaps about 1499–1500, hangs near '*The Virgin of the Rocks*'. Two musical angels nearby, by another painter, probably formed one of the shutters of the Milan altarpiece.

• The angel's face and diaphanous veil are the only areas of 'The Virgin of the Rocks' where Leonardo's intentions were fully carried out. The brush strokes here are firm but delicate, revealing the structure underlying a shimmer of light and shade.

• The blue of the water and furthest rocks illustrates Leonardo's knowledge of aerial perspective as a complement to linear perspective: just as objects appear smaller as they recede into the distance, so colours seem to fade to pale blue the further they are from the viewer.

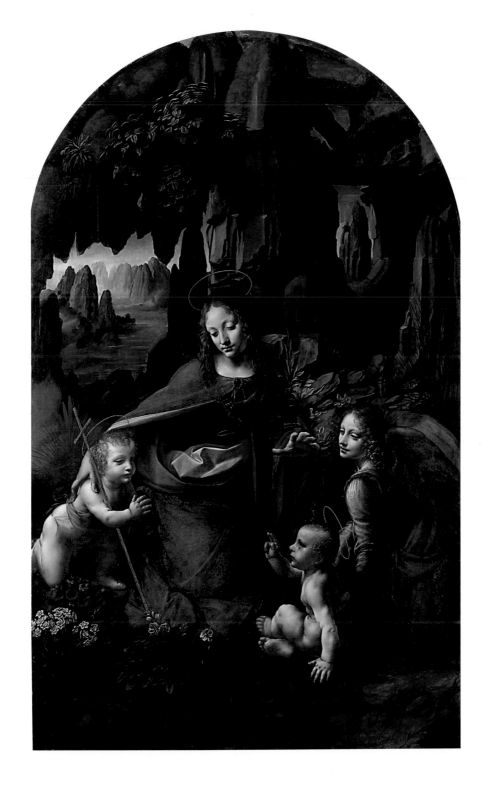

8. **Saint Jerome** (about 1496)

Oil on pearwood   23.1 × 17.4 cm

In 1494 Albrecht Dürer is believed to have undertaken a momentous journey from his native Nuremberg to Venice, crossing the fearful mountain passes of the Alps to discover for himself the art of Italy. For, if German art excelled in fantasy and empirical observation of detail, expressive yet precise line and contour, Italian art seemed to hold the secret of universal harmony. Italian artists had inherited from Graeco-Roman antiquity the ability to portray the nude, and through judiciously proportioned figures in appropriate poses, the use of perspective, light, shade and colour, Italians created unified, emotionally compelling compositions.

The travel sketches Dürer made on his outward journey were mere topographical inventories. Those he made on his return voyage became poetic records of experience. This minute oil painting in its turn transmutes private watercolour studies into a devotional picture for which a buyer could be found. Saint Jerome, heroic penitent and visionary scholar, inhabits, with his companion lion, a wilderness half-way between Germany and Italy. Finches dip into the living waters at his feet, his crucifix is held fast in the stump of a silver birch. Firs crown the jagged crags, and the road winds to a forest of oaks and conifers. From this Germanic gloom the view opens onto an airy Italian plain, beyond which shimmering mountains recede into thin blue air. Made brighter by the black filigree of a leafless tree, the sun's yellow and orange blaze defies the clouds, either dark outriders of the night – or its rearguard retreating as the dawn breaks.

• The pitched slate roofs of a Germanic castle rise up among trees native to northern Europe. The road behind Saint Jerome is a symbol of his spiritual journey, but the picture is also an evocation of Dürer's intellectual development: although broadening his horizons, he remains loyal to his German heritage.

• On the reverse of this panel is a swiftly, summarily painted comet, perhaps a heavenly portent of the Last Judgment. Jerome, while in penitence in the wilderness, is said to have heard the trumpet heralding Christ's Second Coming, as predicted in the Book of Revelation, also known as the Apocalypse.

• Saint Jerome (?347–420) compiled the standard Latin translation of the Bible, the Vulgate. Although the office of cardinal was unknown in his day, as a papal adviser he was posthumously 'promoted' to it, and is usually shown with a cardinal's broad-brimmed red hat and cloak.

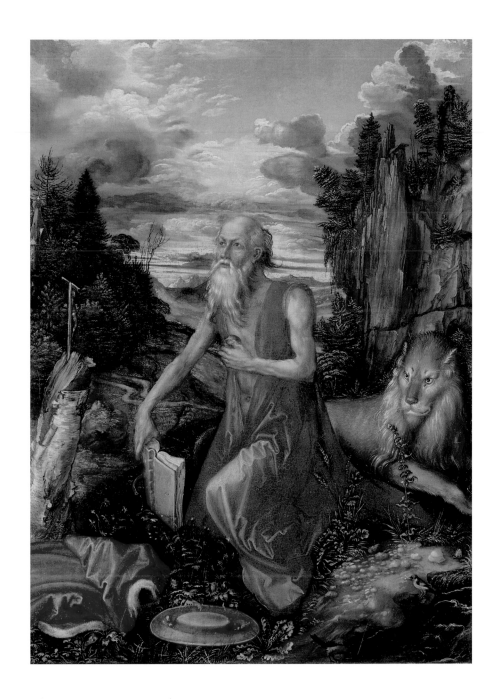

FROM HOLBEIN TO VERONESE
Paintings 1500–1600

Lined with richly coloured fabrics, the walls of the West Wing resemble those of the princely palaces for which many of the works assembled here were painted.

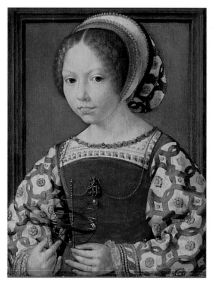

Fig.1 **Jan Gossaert** *A Little Girl,* about 1520

Most of the pictures appear larger, or at least more imposing and more animated, than those in the Sainsbury Wing, and there are more portraits and more references to pagan antiquity here. Veronese's *The Family of Darius before Alexander* may combine both, to flatter the family whose palace it once adorned. As in a great *tableau vivant,* members of the clan re-enact a fabled moment in ancient history, celebrating the pagan – even un-Christian – virtues of male comradeship and courtly magnanimity. Untroubled by the Christian prohibition of suicide, Lotto's *Portrait of a Lady inspired by Lucretia* proclaims her kinship with a celebrated ancient Roman heroine who killed herself to preserve her virtue. In general, Italian artists in the West Wing seem more comfortable with such subjects than northern European ones, for it was in Italy that Graeco-Roman statues were now being eagerly excavated, and manuscripts of Greek and Latin authors rediscovered, to be collected by classically educated grandees. Titian was inspired both by ancient sculpture and poetry when he painted *Bacchus and Ariadne* for a book-loving, military-commander prince, as was Bronzino in the stylish, but more explicitly erotic, *An Allegory with Venus and Cupid.*

But the revival of pagan antiquity did not preclude a continued interest in Christian art.

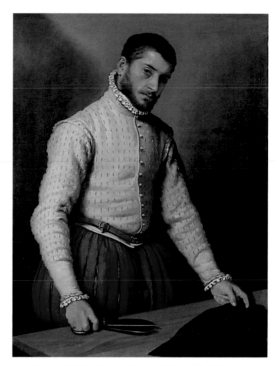

Fig.2 **Giovanni Battista Moroni** *Portrait of a Man ('The Tailor'),* about 1570

Altarpieces were still required. In central Italy they were now more often painted on a single panel, replacing the complex, many panelled structures of earlier centuries. Michelangelo's unfinished *Entombment* shows, in the perfectly proportioned body of the dead Christ, the artist's youthful ideal of beauty as derived from ancient sculpture – and indeed the painting itself resembles sculpture, Michelangelo's preferred medium.

Portraits in the West Wing often give the illusion of revealing the sitters' characters, their inner life (figs 1 and 2). Raphael's *Julius II* was said to terrify those who came into its presence, as if it had been the man himself. Cranach's *Johann Friedrich the Magnanimous*, although a small half-length likeness, captures all the nervous energy of a six-year-old. Holbein's *'Ambassadors',* shown surrounded by emblems of their worldly accomplishments, gravely meditate on eternity.

Oil painting gradually replaced egg tempera throughout Italy; it reached its apogee in Venice, in the works of Titian and Veronese. A great maritime power, the city had a highly developed shipbuilding industry, and her artists increasingly turned from panel to canvas, the cloth used for sails. As Titian matured, his oil technique became bolder and more expressive; combined with the rough texture of the canvas, the trace of the artist's gesture with brush and fingers enlivens the surface of his late pictures. Because canvas, which can be rolled up, is more easily transported than wooden panels, Titian, working from Venice, was able to supply paintings to royal patrons abroad. His paintings, dispersed throughout Europe, were to influence Western artists everywhere, for centuries to come.

9. The Entombment (about 1500–1)

Oil on wood   161.7 × 149.9 cm

This poignant Entombment is almost certainly an altarpiece. The young Michelangelo is known to have begun in it September 1500 for a funerary chapel in Rome, and abandoned it in the spring of 1501. In its original setting, Christ's body, lifted up to be carried to the tomb, would have appeared as if it were being lowered onto the altar below the painting, where Christians believe it is transformed into the Eucharist, the 'living bread' of Holy Communion. Michelangelo blocked out the figures first, like sculptures, then laid in the landscape background. Christ's body, as cold and smooth as marble, is the only nearly finished area of the painting, although even at this late stage of completion the wounds in the feet and side are not shown. He is carried by Joseph of Arimathea, the vermilion-clad Saint John the Evangelist and, probably, one of the Virgin Mary's attendants. The kneeling woman below Saint John was meant to be shown meditating on the crown of thorns and the nails of the Crucifixion. The missing figure on the right was to be the Virgin Mary, mourning her Son. Michelangelo was awaiting delivery of the costly blue pigment lapis lazuli, or ultramarine, traditionally used for her cloak, when he was called away to return to Florence.

MICHELANGELO IN
THE NATIONAL GALLERY

Another unfinished painting, *The Virgin and Child with Saint John and Angels*, called '*The Manchester Madonna*' as it was exhibited in Manchester in 1857, is also generally believed to be a work by the young Michelangelo, dating from about 1497. Unlike *The Entombment*, it is painted in tempera.

• The white silhouette of the tomb and surrounding small figures was reinforced by scraping or pushing away the still-wet brown paint of the rocks – the technique of a sculptor more accustomed to chipping away material rather than adding it.

• The appearance of this picture has altered due to chemical changes in some pigments. Michelangelo painted the dress of the Mary supporting Christ with brilliant pale green in the highlights and bright emerald green in the shadows. Its present colour is caused by the discoloration of a thin unifying glaze of a once-green copper compound.

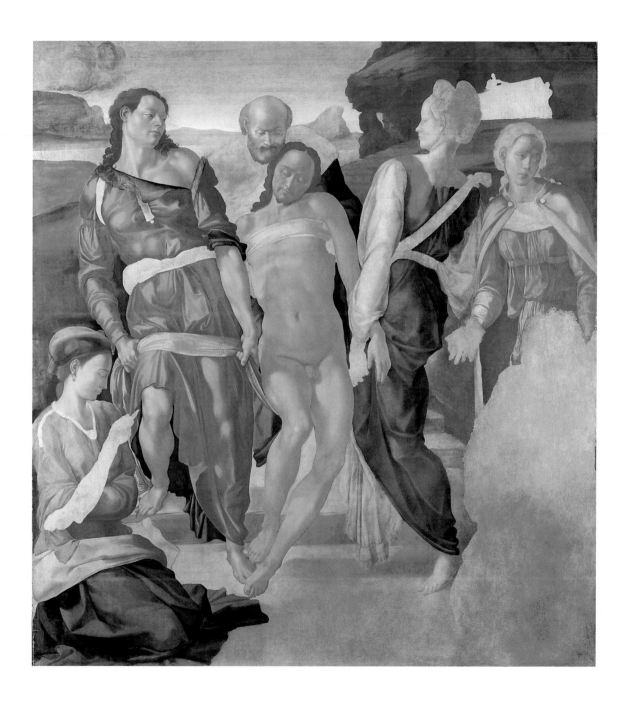

10. **Pope Julius II** (1511–12)

Oil on wood   108 × 80.7 cm

A contemporary reported of this portrait that 'it was so lifelike and true that it frightened everyone who saw it, as if it were the living man himself.' The turbulent Julius II personally led the papal battalions on strenuous military campaigns. Mortified at having lost the city of Bologna in 1511, he grew a beard, which he shaved off by March 1512 – thus usefully enabling us to date Raphael's painting. The picture has been so influential, so widely copied, that its novelty may escape us. By turning the pope's armchair sideways, and his gaze inwards, Raphael has transformed the official image of an enthroned ruler – like those on coins, medals and seals – into a penetrating study of character. It is, in addition, beautifully painted in a Venetian-influenced colour harmony of red and green, white and gold. The pattern of papal keys and triple crowns just visible in the green curtain was originally painted gold to simulate brocade or embroidery. The artist's change of mind, discovered when the picture was examined in 1969 prior to cleaning, is one of the main reasons for it being accepted as the original of several versions of the portrait.

RAPHAEL IN
THE NATIONAL GALLERY

The Collection contains paintings from virtually every stage of Raphael's short career: from early works influenced by Perugino (*The Crucified Christ with the Virgin Mary, Saints and Angels*, about 1503) and Florentine pictures indebted to Leonardo (*Saint Catherine of Alexandria*, about 1507–8) to this mature portrait of his greatest Roman patron.

• The pope's bejewelled hands are a clue to his volatile character. The left, foreshortened hand forcefully grips the arm of the chair. The right hand is relaxed, holding an aristocratic, and costly, cambric handkerchief.

• The bronze acorns adorning the papal armchair are personal emblems: Julius's family name was della Rovere, the Italian word for 'oak'. The reflections of the window – the source of light – and the pope's crimson cap demonstrate how thoroughly Raphael had by this time absorbed the techniques of oil painting imported to Italy from the Netherlands.

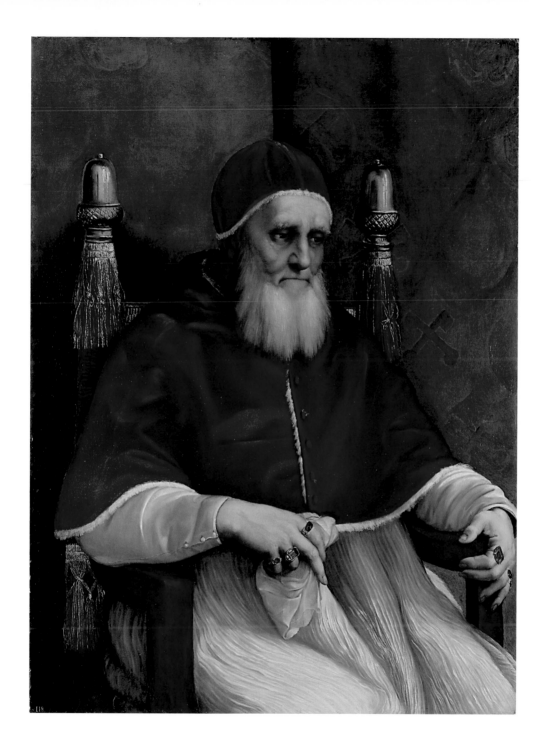

11. Johann the Steadfast and Johann Friedrich the Magnanimous (1509)

Oil on wood 41.3 × 31 cm and 42 × 31.2 cm

The Electors of Saxony – German princes entitled to take part in the election of the Holy Roman Emperor – were the patrons of Luther; they were also fortunate in their choice of court painter. Lucas Cranach became the chief artist of the Reformation, and portrayed its main protagonists, including Luther himself. In this double portrait of the Elector Johann the Steadfast and his heir Johann Friedrich, however, he seems simply to have seized the opportunity to paint one of the earliest and most sympathetic portraits of a child in European art. The paintings break with the tradition of paired portraits of husband and wife, probably because the boy's mother, Sophia of Mecklenburg, died giving birth to him in 1503. While the father's likeness is based on a drawing made some time before, the child's seems so spontaneous that it must have been taken especially for this picture, perhaps the six-year-old's first formal engagement. Shown full-face, he looks out with a shy yet proud sidelong glance from beneath the fantastical ostrich plumes of his hat. The placing of his head higher than his father's and the greater area of paint devoted to his elaborate costume suggest his small size: a little boy perched on a tall stool to face adult scrutiny.

CRANACH IN
THE NATIONAL GALLERY
Mythology and the nude were new themes Cranach introduced at court, exemplified by *The Close of the Silver Age?*, 1527–35, and *Cupid Complaining to Venus*, probably early 1530s. The allegorical figure of Charity, 1537–50, is also nude, but her little girl carries a doll dressed in contemporary costume.

• The ostrich feathers on Johann Friedrich's hat are painted in bold, three-dimensional swirls, and in places Cranach has used the end of his brush to scratch lines in the wet paint. These vigorous techniques subtly suggest the lively character of the sitter; the raised paint also contrasts with the smooth, delicate handling of the flesh tones.

• Where the ornamental slashing reveals the red lining of Johann Friedrich's green outer garment, Cranach has left firm three-dimensional ridges of paint. It was customary for the sitter to pose first for a rapid drawing of his face, and for his clothes to be modelled on a mannequin and painted at leisure 'from life'.

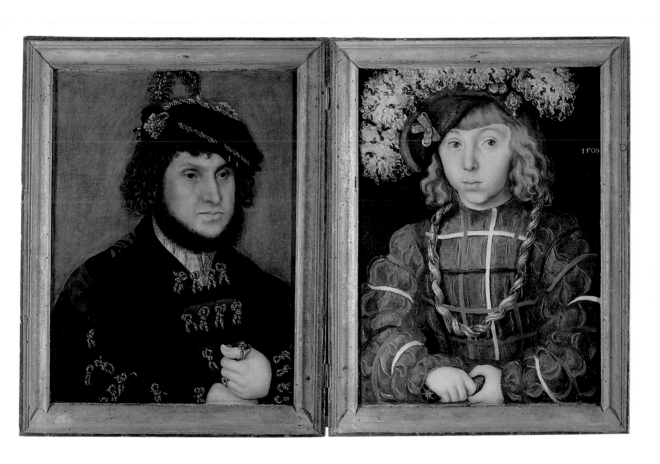

12. **Bacchus and Ariadne** (1521–3)

Oil on canvas 172.2 × 188.3 cm

This is without doubt the noisiest picture in the National Gallery – and never before had pagan myth been brought to life so vividly. Inspired by extracts from ancient Latin poems sent him by his patron, Alfonso d'Este of Ferrara, Titian pictures the moment when the god of wine Bacchus, returning from India with his rowdy retinue of goat-footed satyrs and maenads, encounters a disconsolate Ariadne abandoned on Naxos by her ungrateful lover Theseus. On the isle's 'wave-sound shore … cymbals resound and drums beaten by frenzied hands', a cacophony joined by the barking of Titian's own little dog in the foreground. The god leaps impetuously from his chariot to ravish the frightened girl: she will become his celestial bride, the constellation we see in the sky above her.

The painting was one of several made for Alfonso's study, where he wished to re-create an ancient picture gallery – probably imaginary – described in a late-antique Greek text. For this special commission, Titian has used an unusually wide variety of pigments, such as orange realgar and yellow orpiment, available mainly in Venice.

TITIAN IN
THE NATIONAL GALLERY
Titian is represented in the National Gallery with great works from throughout his life: religious paintings (*Noli me Tangere*, probably 1510–5); individual and group portraits (*Portrait of a Man*, about 1512; *The Vendramin Family*, 1543–7), and a late, unfinished mythological picture, *The Death of Acteon*, about 1565.

• The flower beneath the hooves of the strutting faun trailing a mangled calf's head in the foreground is the flower of the caper plant, which in reality grows only in the crevices of rocks and walls. It is a symbol of love. Titian imagines a violent and alluring pagan world, uninhibited by Christian morality.

• The cheetahs drawing Bacchus' chariot may be portraits of actual animals in Alfonso d'Este's menagerie. In ancient mythology, Bacchus is accompanied by leopards on his return from India – but all the big cats, tigers included, are meant to be tamed by drinking the god's gift to earthlings: wine.

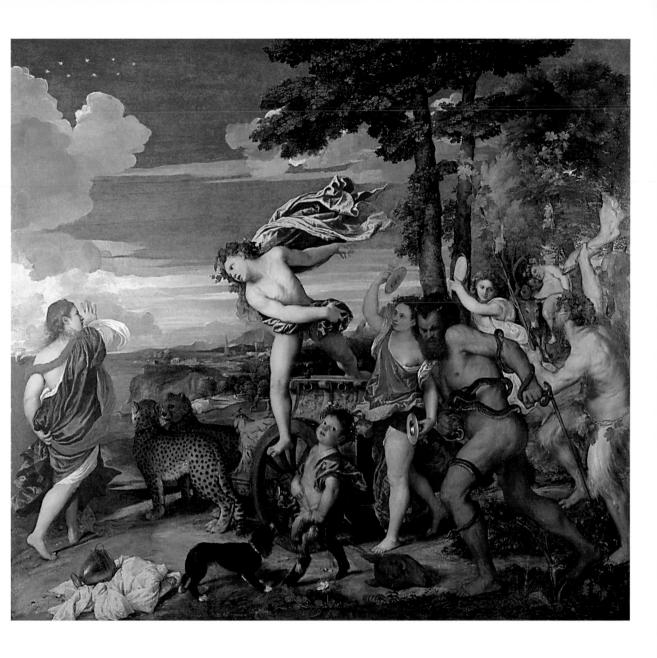

13. **Portrait of a Woman inspired by Lucretia** (about 1530–2)

Oil on canvas, transferred from wood   91.5 × 105.6 cm

Lotto often made punning allusions to his sitters' identity. The unknown Venetian lady sternly gazing out at the viewer was probably named Lucrezia, for she points to a drawing of Lucretia, an ancient Roman heroine who stabbed herself rather than endure the dishonour of having been raped, and thus made unfaithful to her husband. Most portraits are vertical in shape; this unusual horizontal format was frequently used by Lotto, enabling him to include a landscape framed by a window behind or beside the sitter. Here, the shadow cast on the wall suggests that a window, the source of light within the picture, is in the viewer's space in front and to the right of the canvas. Thanks to her forceful gesture and her showy costume, the sitter herself assertively fills most of the picture's surface area. Her face, placed in the centre, is the apex of a bulky pyramid, and the impression of a bold and dynamic personality, calm in the face of potential threats to *her* virtue, is reinforced by another compositional device: a strong diagonal running implicitly from the bottom left to the top right corner of the canvas.

• Lorenzo Lotto was one of the most eccentric and original artists of the Italian High Renaissance. A Venetian by birth and training, he also found inspiration in Northern European art. The altarpieces he painted in Bergamo, in the foothills of the Alps, were later, in turn, to influence the Flemish artist Rubens.

• The drawing of Lucretia is of course, like the rest of the picture, painted in oils, but it cleverly gives the illusion of a drawing in ink and wash on paper. The nudity of the figure would once have made her instantly recognisable as a personage from ancient Roman myth or history.

• Lucretia's story was told in the Latin writer Livy's *History of Rome*, (I: 58) quoted in Roman script on the piece of paper on the table, 'Nor shall ever unchaste woman live, following the example of Lucretia.' The wallflower may be a reference to the mythological rape of Persephone by Hades, god of the underworld, but it was also used as a simple love token.

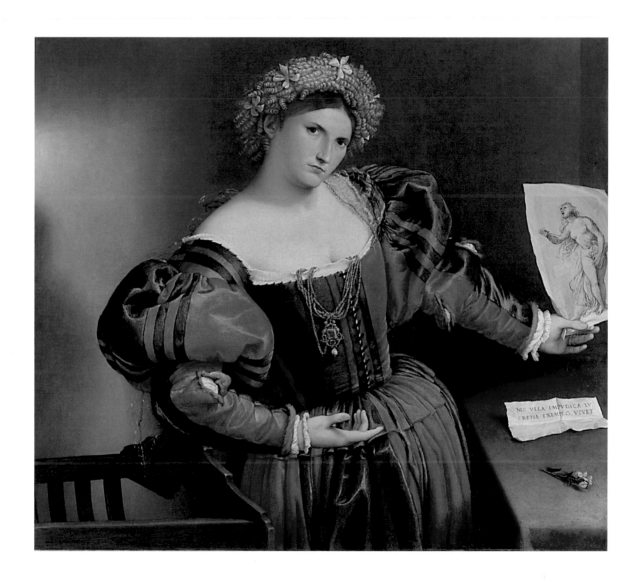

NEC VLLA IMPVDICA LV
CRETIA EXEMPLO VIVET

14. 'The Ambassadors' (1533)

Oil on oak   207 × 209.5 cm

This huge panel, with its extraordinary array of still-life objects and an optical puzzle in the foreground, is one of the earliest surviving portraits to include two large full-length figures. It celebrates the friendship and accomplishments of Jean de Dinteville (29), French ambassador to England, on the left, and his fellow countryman, Georges de Selve (25), Bishop of Lavaur, who visited him in London in 1533. The two friends exemplify, respectively, the active and the contemplative life, which complement each other. On shelves behind them Holbein depicted their wide-ranging interests – a compendium of the culture of the age.

But a string of the lute has snapped – a traditional emblem of life's fragility. Spread across the mosaic floor at their feet is the distorted shape of a skull: a hidden reminder of death that can only be seen correctly when viewed either from the side of the panel or through a special telescopic device. The hymnal in front of the lute is open at Luther's hymn, 'Come Holy Spirit our souls inspire.' Just visible in the top left corner is a crucifix. When death puts an end to worldly glory, and dust returns to dust, faith in Christ offers the hope of eternal life.

HOLBEIN IN
THE NATIONAL GALLERY
Holbein is represented in the Gallery by four major portraits; one of Erasmus is on loan. The other two are a full-length likeness of Christina of Denmark, widowed Duchess of Milan, painted for King Henry VIII probably in about 1538, and the half-length of the unknown *Lady with a Squirrel and a Starling*, about 1526–8.

• Holbein distorted a drawing of a skull through a geometric process called anamorphosis. When viewed at a corrective angle, either from the side or reflected in a metal cylinder, the skull is restored to a normal appearance.

• The terrestrial globe on the lower shelf has been 'customised' so that in the centre of the map of France we read the name of Polisy, Jean de Dinteville's château, which is not found on contemporary globes otherwise similar to this. The map of the world depicted here has been related to one published in Nuremberg in 1523.

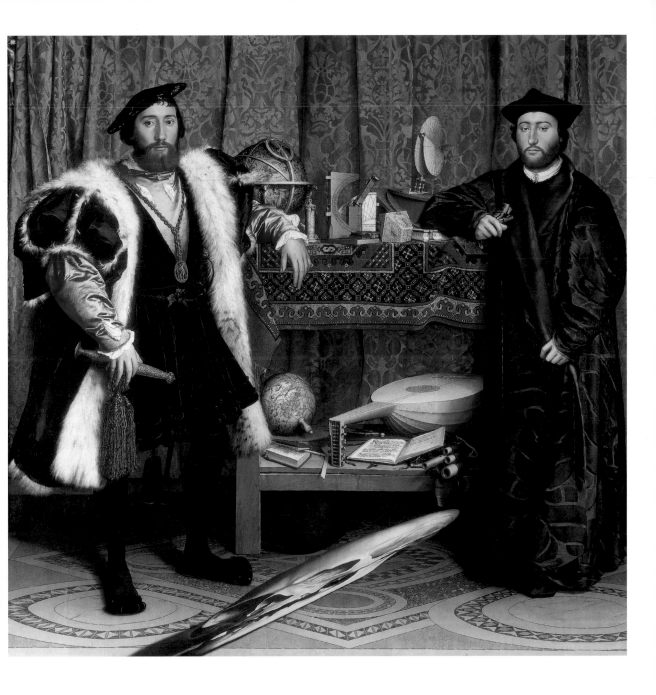

15. **An Allegory with Venus and Cupid** (probably 1540–50)

Oil on wood   146.5 × 116.8 cm

Bronzino's *Allegory* attracts and repels in equal proportion: it is perhaps the coolest, most aloof, least sensuous and yet most overtly erotic depiction of sexual passion ever painted. Made at the court of Duke Cosimo I de'Medici in Florence, it was possibly a present to Francis I of France; unravelling its complex symbolism would have offered bored courtiers the perfect opportunity to dwell pleasurably on the charms of Venus and Cupid, and the lubricious details of their embrace. Foolish Pleasure, the laughing child with an anklet of bells, strews rose petals over the lovers, heedless of the thorn piercing his foot. Behind him Deceit, fair of face but foul of body, proffers a sweet honeycomb in one hand, concealing the scorpion's sting in her tail with the other. On the other side is a dark tormented figure, perhaps Jealousy but more likely Pain or Suffering (possibly related to syphilis, the epidemic venereal disease newly introduced into Europe and treated with poisonous mercury). Oblivion, the figure on the upper left, attempts to draw a veil over the scene, but is prevented by Father Time. Alluring at first sight, the image slowly reveals its bitter moral.

• Bronzino, who also painted religious works, excelled in portraiture. He painted all the members of Duke Cosimo's family, and while his adult portraits are as sophisticated, elegant and remote as this *Allegory*, his likenesses of children are lively and expressive.

• Contrasting masks of comedy and tragedy were often represented in ancient Graeco-Roman art, but these masks look more like the faces of a nymph and a satyr – in pagan mythology, the prey and predator of sexual conquest.

• Oblivion is not a mask: only the back of her head is missing. According to phrenology, the pseudo-science which studies people's mental faculties through the shape of their cranium, this is where memory is stored. Bronzino's allegorical figures are partly traditional, like those of Time and Foolish Pleasure, and partly invented or adapted from other sources.

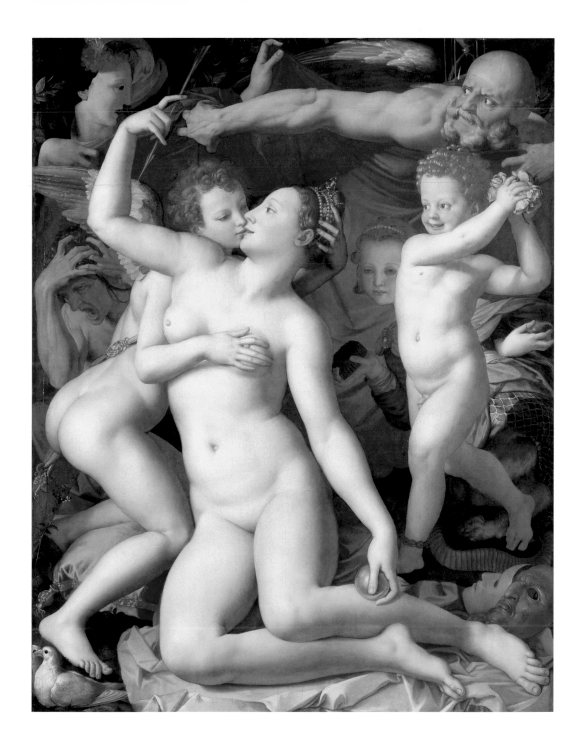

16. **The Family of Darius before Alexander** (1565–70)

Oil on canvas 236.2 × 474.9 cm

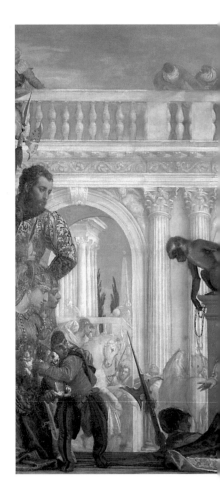

Paolo Caliari, known as 'Veronese' after his birth place of Verona, become one of the leading artists of Venice. Thanks to his sumptuous decorative paintings for the city's churches and palaces, Venetian Renaissance life is often imagined as a succession of stately pageants in fancy dress, unfolding against white marble and blue skies. This imposing canvas, however, perhaps painted for a family palace in celebration of a marriage, depicts an exemplary episode from ancient history. Alexander the Great, having defeated the Persian King Darius, treated his foe's mother, wife and children with magnanimity. When he went to visit them with his general and dearest friend, Hephaestion, the Queen Mother, Sisygambis, misled by Hephaestion's greater height, prostrated herself before him. Alexander courteously forgave her, saying, 'It is no mistake, for he too is an Alexander.' The pointing gestures of the elderly courtier and Sisygambis probably refer to the painting's secon-dary theme, Alexander's epoch-making 'continence' or sexual self-restraint: contrary to the normal conqueror's practice of his day, he abstained from making Darius's beautiful wife his concubine. Some of Veronese's figures, such as Alexander, Hephaestion and the Queen Mother, may be portraits, probably of members of the patrons' family.

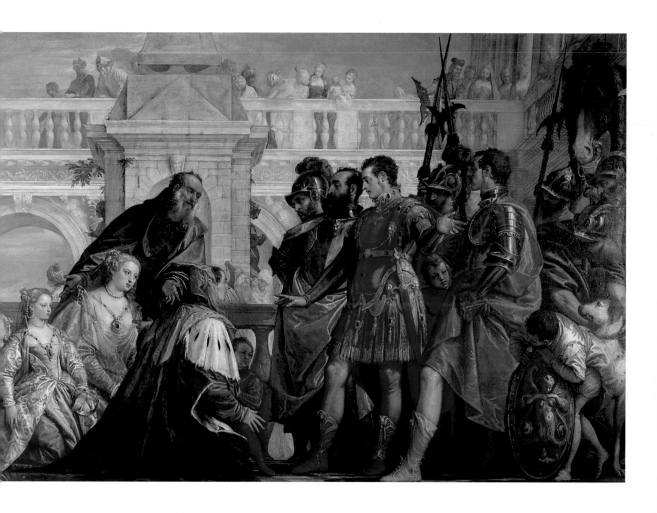

• Veronese painted the background first. The carefully grouped figures in the foreground, in order to appear nearer to the viewer, were finished in bolder colours and with denser paint. But he later added some horses in a gap between the figures. As oil paint becomes translucent with age, the architecture has again become visible through the thinly painted horses.

• The Queen Mother's page boy demonstrates how the artist achieved his celebrated effect of luminous daylight. Reversing pictorial convention, Veronese placed the child's bright, saturated red costume behind the Queen's dark cape – suggesting to the viewer that bright sunlight is reflected even in the shade. The cape's white ermine collar 'pushes back' the boy from the foreground.

FROM CARAVAGGIO TO VERMEER
Paintings 1600–1700

A kind of artistic explosion took place in the seventeenth century. New centres of painting arose, new clients bought pictures and new subjects were painted. The novelties are most noticeable in the many Dutch works in the North Wing.

Here we find river scenes and seascapes and, in paintings like Cuyp's *River Landscape with Horseman and Peasants*, landscapes inhabited not by saints but by cattle and milkmaids, hunters and horsemen. There are also townscapes, church interiors (fig.1), lush paintings of flowers and fruit, still lifes (fig.2) and portrayals of women and children busied in the neat interiors of Dutch houses – such as de Hooch's *Courtyard of a House in Delft* and Vermeer's *A Young Woman standing at a Virginal*. It is as if Dutch artists had suddenly opened their eyes to the world around them. And that, in a way, is what had happened. The Dutch Republic, emancipated from Spanish rule, adopted Calvinism as its official religion. Since

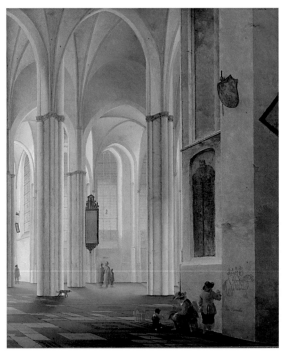

Fig.1 **Pieter Saenredam** *The Interior of the Buurkerk at Utrecht*, 1664

the Protestant Calvin had prohibited the use of images in worship, Dutch artists lost the patronage of the Church, and had to find other clients. Luckily, patriotism and growing prosperity combined to stimulate a demand for paintings of local scenes for private houses. And even when religious subjects were pictured, they were usually

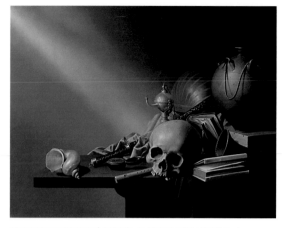

Fig.2 **Harmen Steenwyck** *Still Life: An Allegory of the Vanities of Human Life*, about 1640

made for domestic use – Protestants, unlike Roman Catholics, were encouraged to read the Bible in their own language at home. Scenes from both the New Testament and the Hebrew Bible were painted, as examples of righteous behaviour or as warnings: Rembrandt's *Belshazzar's Feast*, probably intended for a dining room, alludes to the fearful consequences of desecrating holy things and worshipping false gods.

Innovation was not confined to the Protestant north. In Catholic Rome, Caravaggio, with works such as *The Supper at Emmaus*, forged a new, dramatic realism – a dark vision that affected painting throughout Europe. The Italian's was not the only influence, however, and while we can trace it in works such as Rubens's nocturnal *Samson and Delilah*, the Flemish painter-diplomat – during his long stay in Italy – looked just as closely at sixteenth-century and ancient art: innovation can result from rediscovery. Rubens, on his visit to Madrid, opened Velázquez's eyes to the works of Titian in the Spanish royal collection – so that the young Spaniard, whose early paintings owed most to Caravaggio, came to emulate the colourism and free brush work of the great Venetian, as illustrated by '*The Rokeby Venus*'. But perhaps the most ardent seventeenth-century champion of Titian was Van Dyck, a Flemish Catholic and once Rubens's assistant,

best remembered for his brilliant portraits of English royalists like *Lord John Stuart and his Brother, Lord Bernard Stuart*. It was also the rediscovery of Titian, as much as of ancient Roman wall painting, which prompted the French artist Poussin's poetic visions of pagan rites in *A Bacchanalian Revel before a Term of Pan*.

Poussin's friend and compatriot, Claude Lorrain, evolved a new kind of landscape and coastal scene. These paintings introduce a new theme: the northern European's longing for the sunlit south, all Europe's nostalgia for a Golden Age.

17. **The Supper at Emmaus** (1601)

Oil and egg on canvas   141 × 196.2 cm

This is one of Caravaggio's earliest representations of biblical history as current event. Two shabby travellers – one wears the scallop-shell badge of a pilgrim – have invited a third, whom they met on the road, to share their meal. When he blesses the bread in the inn at Emmaus, they recognise their crucified Lord, Jesus Christ, risen from the dead (Luke 24: 13-31). We are made witnesses of the miraculous event – virtually included in the scene, as the basket of fruit on the edge of the table threatens to tip over in our laps. The chair and the torn sleeve of the disciple on the left, and the left hand of the disciple on the right, seem to project from the picture surface into our space. Caravaggio brought with him to Rome lessons learnt in his native Lombardy: the dramatic spotlighting derives from Leonardo's use of light and shade, while the composition recalls the central scene of his *Last Supper* in Milan, translated into a realistic idiom derived from German art. Christ, however, is beardless, like Michelangelo's Christ in the Sistine Chapel *Last Judgment* (1537-42?).

CARAVAGGIO IN
THE NATIONAL GALLERY
The artist's early Roman works, like *Boy bitten by a Lizard*, 1595–1600, combine still lifes of fruit and flowers with a single figure in a quasi-erotic pose. From 1600, he mainly painted religious subjects, increasingly harsh and summary in technique: such as *Salome receives the Head of Saint John the Baptist*, 1607–10.

• The basket of fruit is typical of Caravaggio's early manner. It is remarkable not only for the perspectival illusion of balancing precariously at the edge of the table, but also for the realism of its imposing arrangement of fruit. These are drawn from several seasons and mottled and worm-eaten, perhaps to symbolise sin and death, conquered by Christ.

• The outstretched left hand that, artfully foreshortened, seems to project into our space, appears larger than the disciple's right hand, emphasising the illusion of abrupt recession; the dramatic gesture of both arms, parallel to the brightly lit edge of the white tablecloth, is like an arrow pointing straight to the figure of Christ.

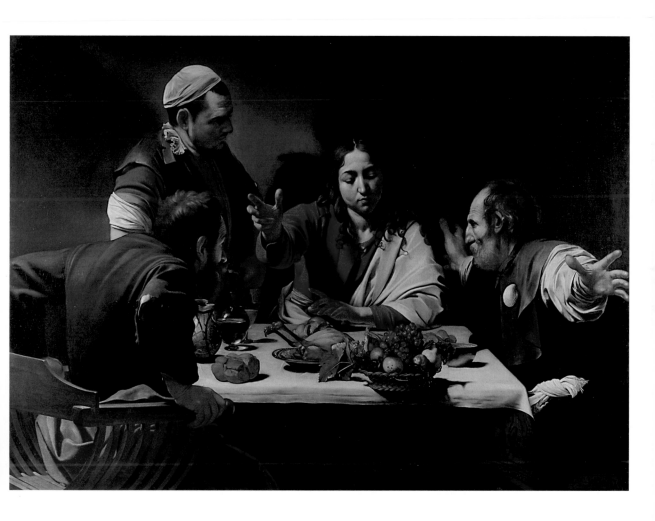

18. **Belshazzar's Feast** (about 1636–8)

Oil on canvas 167.6 × 209.2 cm

This dramatic scene illustrates chapter five of the Old Testament Book of Daniel. Belshazzar, King of Babylon, gave a great feast at which wine was drunk from the gold and silver vessels looted by his father, Nebuchadnezzar, from the temple at Jerusalem, and pagan gods were worshipped instead of God. At the height of the feast a hand appeared writing mysterious words on the wall, which only the Jewish sage Daniel was able to interpret. They foretold the defeat – indeed, death – of Belshazzar that same night, and the partition of his kingdom among the Medes and Persians. Rembrandt, who could not have seen Caravaggio's *Supper at Emmaus* but was influenced by the Italian artist's Dutch followers, has imagined a strikingly similar composition, of dramatically lit half-figures assembled around a table. As he rises in terror, Belshazzar's gold chain sways convulsively, an unseen light source in front of the picture casting its dark shadow on the King's robe; a bright supernatural light also emanates from the inscription. Rembrandt's turbulent effects were exaggerated when, years later, the canvas was trimmed and re-stretched at an angle, so that the table now runs uphill, and the spilt wine falls sideways rather than vertically.

REMBRANDT IN
THE NATIONAL GALLERY
There are some twenty paintings by Rembrandt in the National Gallery: they include his *Self Portrait at the Age of 34*, 1640, and *Self Portrait at the Age of 63*, 1669; a portrait of his first wife, *Saskia van Uylenburgh in Arcadian Costume*, 1635, and of his companion, *Portrait of Hendrickje Stoffels*, 1654–6.

• The writing on the wall spells out the Aramaic words MENE MENE TEKEL UPHARSIN in Hebrew letters. Biblical scholars puzzled over why none but Daniel should have been able to read them. Rembrandt has followed his friend Menasseh ben Israel's suggestion, that the Hebrew letters were written vertically from top to bottom as well as from right to left.

• Heavy encrustations of yellow and white paint – worked while wet – with pale lines scratched with the end of the brush, form Belshazzar's dazzling brocade cloak. The dark, nocturnal tonality of the whole picture is due to Rembrandt's use of a dark grey underpaint, sometimes left visible and sometimes covered only by a translucent dark glaze.

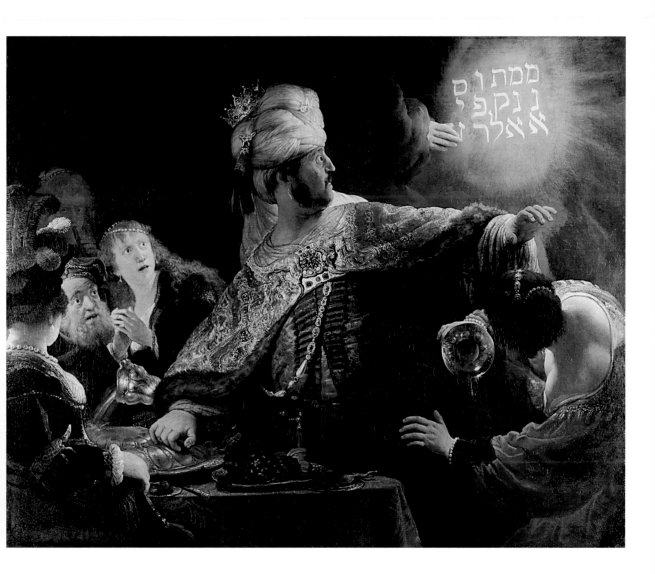

19. A Bacchanalian Revel before a Term of Pan (1630–4)

Oil on canvas 99.7 × 142.9 cm

More through determination than natural talent, Poussin, the unlearned son of a Norman tanner, became Poussin the Roman 'painter-philosopher'. This canvas is one of several inspired by Titian's pictures for Alfonso d'Este (see *Bacchus and Ariadne*), brought to Rome in the early 1620s; it also demonstrates Poussin's study of ancient sculpture and vase paintings representing pagan rites. Nymphs and shepherds dance drunkenly before a wreathed figure of Pan or Priapus, deities of woodlands and gardens, associated with Bacchus, god of wine. Phallic pillar-statues like these were set in Roman gardens as emblems of fertility; Bacchus himself, like the grape vine, symbolised the springtime rebirth of nature. A satyr embraces a laughing nymph. Another nymph, her nose a toper's red, squeezes out a bunch of grapes, the juice falling as wine into the cup of two staggering little putti – bacchic revellers often carved on Roman sarcophagi to signify immortality. Like Titian, Poussin sets the figures against a distant background, partly screened by trees, of sky and airy blue vistas. In imitation of classical reliefs, he shows the dancers at a supposedly static moment, before their feet descend again to strike the ground.

POUSSIN IN
THE NATIONAL GALLERY
Poussin reused the central group, reversed, in the more solemn dance of *The Adoration of the Golden Calf*, 1634–5. The National Gallery houses some ten paintings by the artist, including religious scenes like *The Adoration of the Shepherds*, about 1634, and *The Annunciation*, 1657.

• The satyr may represent Pan himself, half-human and half-goat in shape, a primitive and lustful deity often contrasted in ancient art with the sun god Apollo, who typified high culture. A god of flocks and herds rather than agriculture, and associated with wild and remote places, Pan could make humans, like cattle, stampede in 'panic' terror.

• The grapes held by the drunken nymph, and the juice squeezed out of them, help to 'detach' the foreground from the pale blue distant background. This device of a darker shape set against the sky is called a *repoussoir*, from the French 'to push away'.

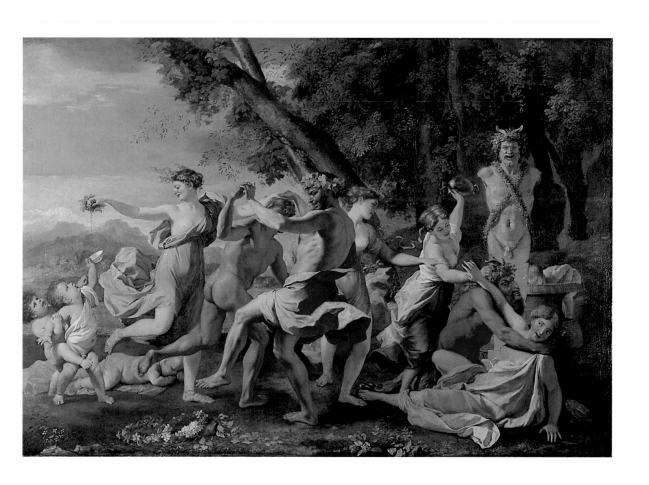

20. **Samson and Delilah** (1609)

Oil on wood   185 × 205 cm

The story of Samson's betrayal is told in the Old Testament (Judges 16:4–6; 16–21). Bribed by his Philistine enemies, Delilah seduces the infatuated Jewish hero into revealing the source of his superhuman strength: his long hair. Here, as he lies asleep in her lap after a night of lovemaking, she calls in a barber to cut off 'the seven locks of his head'. Soldiers are entering to take him prisoner and blind him. Rubens painted this shortly after his return home to Antwerp after eight years spent in Italy. Made to hang over the mantelpiece in his friend Nicolaas Rockocx's parlour, where it could be seen by visitors, the picture advertised Rubens's skill in marrying Flemish and Italian traditions. The figures of Samson and Delilah, and the statue of Venus and Cupid in the background, are derived from Michelangelo and antique sculpture, while the multiple light effects on different surfaces are typically Netherlandish (light seemingly reflected from below the panel mimics the flicker of an actual fire in the fireplace). The tale of a man brought low by lust was also a traditional Netherlandish subject, but the large size of the painting, which accomodates life-size figures in the foreground, is associated with Italian art.

RUBENS IN
THE NATIONAL GALLERY

On his return to Flanders, Rubens became the leading northern European painter, employed by the Regents of the Spanish Netherlands and the monarchs of Spain and England, who knighted him, and the Queen Mother of France. The National Gallery owns nearly thirty works either entirely painted by him or in collaboration with his assistants.

• Rubens introduced an old procuress, a traditional figure in Netherlandish painting but not mentioned in the Bible. Her presence here shows that Delilah is a prostitute; but since her profile is an aged version of Delilah's own, it also demonstrates what the treacherous young woman will become when she has aged and lost her beauty.

• The barber cuts Samson's hair with an incongruously dainty professional gesture the artist must have studied from life. A great painter of narrative, Rubens carefully differentiates the reactions of all the characters – from the barber's concentration, to the old procuress's anxious avarice, to Delilah's ambiguous compound of sensuality, triumph and pity.

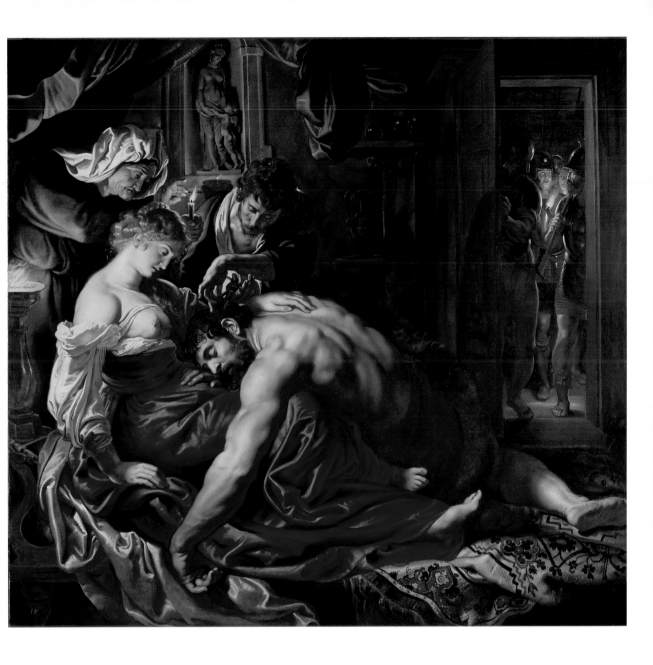

21. Lord John Stuart and his Brother, Lord Bernard Stuart (about 1638)

Oil on canvas   237.5 × 146.1 cm

Early in 1639 the two Stuart brothers, cousins of King Charles I and younger sons of the Duke of Lennox, set off on a three-year tour of the Continent. They must have posed for Van Dyck shortly before their departure. As both were to die a few years later in the Civil War, like so many of Van Dyck's royalist portraits, the picture has gained poignancy with hindsight. Since the Flemish artist's appointment to the English court, he had developed a new portrait formula: the double portrait recording friendship, not necessarily between relations (see 'The Ambassadors'). The two figures are both subtly harmonised and contrasted: Lord John (1621–44), in warm gold and browns, raised slightly as befits the elder, leaning against a pillar, Lord Bernard (1622–45), in cool silver and blue, twisting away from him above the cluster of booted, belaced, befringed legs on the step. Their faces, with the characteristic long Stuart nose, are shown in mirror-image three-quarter views; the diagonal line joining the heads parallels that linking Lord John's right hand with Lord Bernard's left. Van Dyck's compositional skill is surpassed only by his matchless ability to depict satin, lace, kid leather – and aristocratic haughtiness.

• Kid gloves were extremely expensive accessories. Lord Bernard nonchalantly holds his right glove in his gloved left hand – a gesture which allows the painter to suggest the pliant softness of the thin smooth leather. Van Dyck's shimmering brushwork was influenced by his study of Titian. His portrayal of effortless, languid elegance informed the ideal of the 'English gentleman'.

• Lace, gold braid and riding boots were, like gloves, luxurious accessories reserved for the very rich and aristo-cratic. The Stuart brothers are spurred, ready to mount their horses; Lord Bernard's riding boots are shown with an additional, perhaps detachable, flat leather sole – possibly intended to keep the heels from splaying under his weight when he stands.

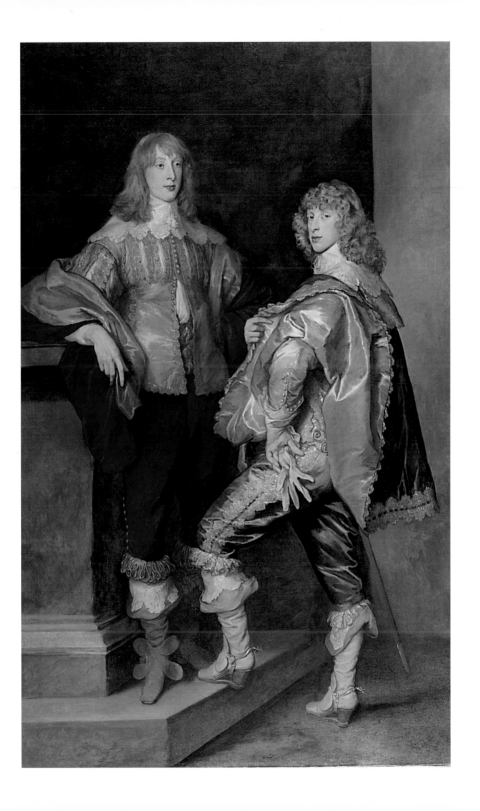

22. The Toilet of Venus ('The Rokeby Venus') (1647–51)

Oil on canvas   122.5 × 177 cm

Although the Spanish royal collection was rich in Venetian Renaissance mythological paintings with naked figures, native Spanish artists, fearful of censure by the Church, rarely represented the female nude. Velázquez is known to have painted only two, and this is the only one to survive, remaining unique in Spanish art for centuries. Obviously indebted to Titian's many versions of 'The Toilet of Venus' and 'Reclining Venus', Velázquez's Venus is nevertheless very different. This picture was almost certainly painted from life, as the model's small waist, jutting hip and modern hair style suggest. Only the presence of the plumply deferential Cupid transforms her into a goddess. The all-pervasive theme of the painting is reflection: Venus reflects on her beauty, which is reflected in the mirror; since the viewer sees the reflection of her face, she must be able to see him (for the painting was certainly intended for a male gaze), and we presume her also to be reflecting on the effect her beauty has on him. Finally, the painter, holding a mirror up to nature, reflects the colours and textures of life in his art.

VELÁZQUEZ IN THE NATIONAL GALLERY
Of the nine works by Velázquez in the National Gallery, one is an early *bodegón* – a picture combining figures with still life – painted in his native Seville, *Kitchen Scene with Christ in the House of Martha and Mary*, probably 1618, and another the famous portrait of *Philip IV of Spain in Brown and Silver*, about 1631–2.

• A single long tapering brushstroke of black paint represents a fold of the satin sheet on which Venus reclines. The black sheet, silvery grey in the highlights, reflects on Venus's rosy skin, which is in turn reflected on the glossy fabric.

• The reflection of Venus's face in the mirror is optically incorrect: as the artist, a student of optics, undoubtedly knew, a real mirror image would have been half the size of the face we see reflected here. Could this image have been intentionally ambiguous: is it a reflection, or a lifelike portrait painted by Velázquez in which Venus sees herself reflected?

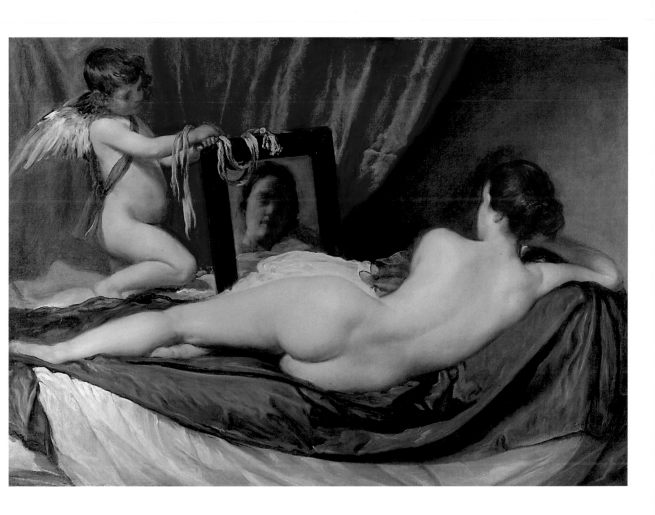

23. Seaport with the Embarkation of Saint Ursula (1641)

Oil on canvas 113 × 149 cm

Claude's idealised landscapes became so influential that they were imitated not only in painting but also in the construction of parks and gardens. The description of his work by Sandrart, a German artist who accompanied him on sketching trips in the countryside outside Rome, cannot be bettered: '[he] only painted, on a small scale, the view from the middle to the greatest distance, fading away towards the horizon and the sky'. Like many of Claude's works, this early morning harbour scene was painted as one of a pair, complementing an afternoon inland vista, now in Hartford, Connecticut. The picture shows the departure, on pilgrimage to Rome, of the legendary Saint Ursula, with her 11,000 virgin companions. They were to be martyred on their return journey through Germany.

CLAUDE IN
THE NATIONAL GALLERY
Claude Gellée, called Lorrain after his birthplace, was the first landscape specialist to achieve international fame. His works, of which the National Gallery has thirteen, were so popular among English eighteenth-century grand tourists to the Continent that many still remain in English country houses.

• The tracery of masts on the ships that will take Ursula and her 11,000 virgin companions to martyrdom makes the sky appear even brighter. Claude's greatest innovation was to harmonise light and space: the entire scene is illuminated only by the rising sun, which almost coincides with the 'vanishing point' on the horizon to which all the lines recede.

• The brilliant saturated blue of the stevedore's breeches in the foreground is the same blue Claude used throughout the painting, for the ships' flags for example, mixing it with increasing quantities of white in proportion with the depth of perspective. The intensity of colour diminishes in exact proportion to the scale of figures and objects.

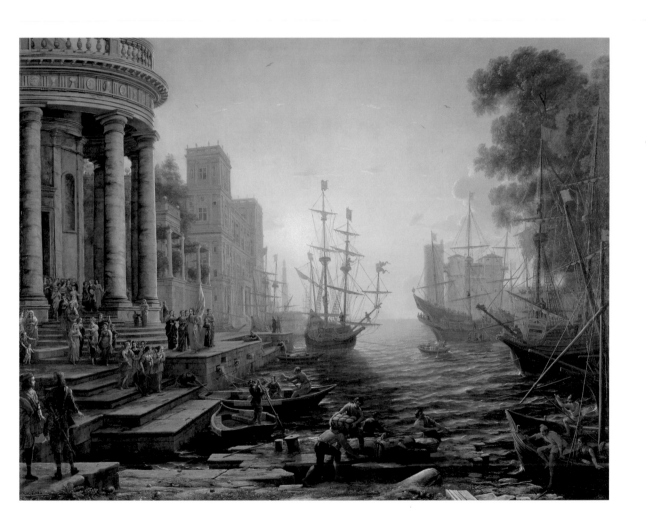

24. **River Landscape with Horseman and Peasants** (probably 1650–60)

Oil on canvas 123 × 241 cm

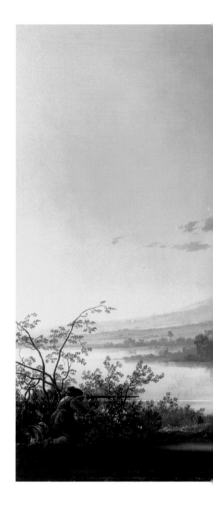

The largest, and probably the finest, of Cuyp's landscapes, this picture may have been designed to be placed high above the wood panelling in a spacious townhouse in Dordrecht, the artist's native city. Cuyp, who had never been to Italy, was influenced by those Dutch artists who had: he bathed the entire scene in the honeyed light of the Italian Campagna – the countryside around Rome immortalised in art by Claude. Other features of this landscape, beside the light, may have seemed exotic to Cuyp's patrons: grandiose mountains that are nowhere to be found in the Low Countries, and a romantic imaginary castle. On the far left, a huntsman is about to shatter for a moment the golden peace of the afternoon. Since hunting was a privilege exclusively reserved for the nobility in the Dutch United Provinces, this detail, like the castle's allusion to feudal grandeur, would have flattered the picture's owners, whether actually noble or merely aspiring to aristocratic status. The picture was the first by Cuyp to enter Britain, in about 1760. Enthusiastically received, it was followed by many others of his best works, decisively influencing the evolution of landscape painting by British artists.

CUYP IN
THE NATIONAL GALLERY

Among Cuyp's eleven paintings in the National Gallery, *The Maas at Dordrecht in a Storm*, about 1645–50, depicts lightning. The picture, seemingly so realistic and of local interest, was almost certainly inspired by the Latin writer Pliny's account of the fabled ancient painter Apelles, who pictured Jupiter's bolts of lightning.

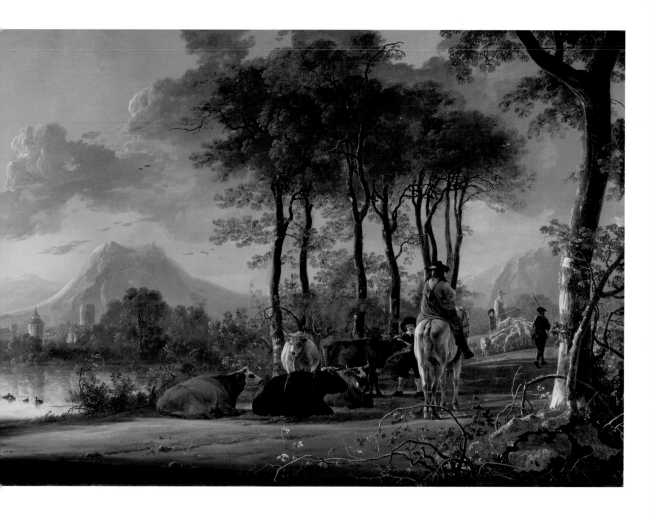

• The horseman surveys his contented flocks and the contented peasants tending them – a reflection of Cuyp's own social aspirations. The favoured artist of Dordrecht's governing classes, he married a wealthy widow. After his marriage he became a deacon of the Reformed Church, took on numerous public offices, and became too grand to devote much time to painting.

• Dairy cattle were a major source of Dutch prosperity, and Cuyp almost invariably included them, often attended by dairy maids with pails of milk, in his idyllic landscapes and views of Dordrecht. Holland was itself sometimes symbolised by a milch cow, associated with peace and plenty.

25. **The Courtyard of a House in Delft** (1658)

Oil on canvas 73.5 × 60 cm

Pieter de Hooch's best-loved pictures, like this one, were painted in Delft, celebrating the homely environment of Dutch burgher women, their children and maidservants, who passed their lives in settings as neatly kept as they were meticulously defined by the artist. Here, he imagined a scene effectively taking place both outdoors and inside, with a tantalising further glimpse through a corridor and across a canal – giving him the opportunity to explore the subtlest variations of natural daylight, and to suggest endless vistas while seemingly depicting only a modest enclosed space. A housewife, silhouetted against the bright wall, directs our gaze along with hers at her neighbours' darkened windows. Pale fawn underpainting lends a warm glow to the entire picture, modulated in the ochre and brick-rose of paving and walls, and the wooden shutter of the barely visible window on the left. The yard and house are old, and the rudimentary trellis ramshackle. The broom, recently used, has fallen into the border as the maid turns her attention to the child, affectionately teaching her by word and example. The inscription on the stone tablet suggests that a life of domestic virtue leads to heaven as surely as more formal religious observance.

• De Hooch's earliest works, painted in his native Rotterdam, depicted guardroom and tavern scenes, peopled with soldiers and serving girls. After 1660, when he moved from Delft to Amsterdam, he specialised in the portrayal of elegant town life, exaggerating the tonal contrast between areas of light and dark in paintings such as *A Musical Party in a Courtyard*, 1677.

• The stone tablet over the archway still exists; it once marked the entrance of the Hieronymusdale cloister. The inscription originally read, 'This is in St Jerome's vale if you wish to retire in meekness and patience. For we must first descend if we wish to be raised.'

• The colour balance planned by de Hooch has altered over time through the fading of yellow and blue pigments. All the foliage in this picture, made up of blue and yellow paint, would once have appeared much greener, the sky bluer and brighter, and the blue of the maid's skirt more intense and less translucent.

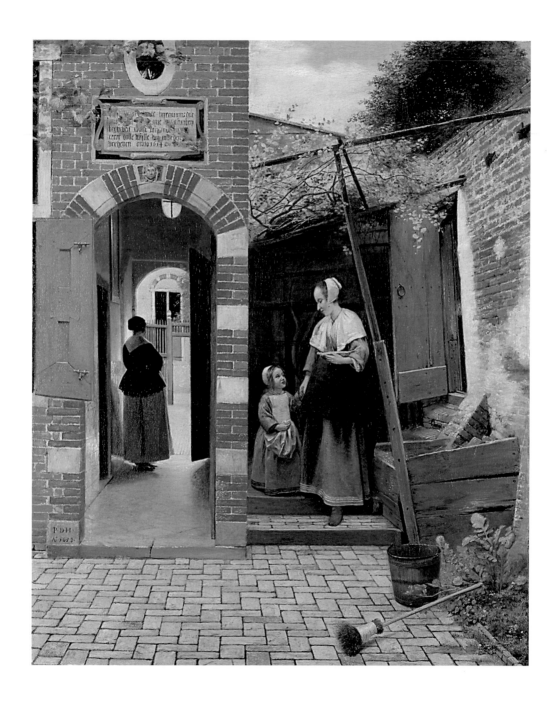

26. A Young Woman standing at a Virginal (about 1670)

Oil on canvas 51.7 × 45.2 cm

Only some thirty-five paintings by Vermeer are known: he worked slowly, ran an inn, held town office in Delft, and practised as an art dealer. Like de Hooch, he is best remembered for small domestic scenes, although he pictured women's leisure more often than their housework. His earliest works were large dramatic narratives, like *Christ in the House of Martha and Mary* (now in Edinburgh), influenced by the Italianate Catholic painters of Utrecht, and he continued to introduce narrative or allegorical significance into paintings of 'everyday life'. The young woman strokes the keys of the virginal – a smaller version of the harpsichord – while looking expectantly out of the canvas. Music is 'the food of love', and the empty chair suggests a partner is missing from the scene, perhaps away travelling abroad among the mountains depicted in the picture on the wall and on the lid of the virginal. Cupid holds up a playing card or tablet in another picture within the picture; contemporary Dutch books of emblems explain the image as a sybol of fidelity in love. The commonplace theme of a girl dreaming of her absent lover is transmuted to great poetry through Vermeer's subtle geometry and serene all-enveloping light.

VERMEER IN
THE NATIONAL GALLERY
Vermeer's *Young Woman Seated at a Virginal*, about 1670, is sometimes said to have been painted as a contrasting pendant to this picture: the painting of a brothel scene on the wall behind the young woman suggests she is motivated by mercenary love.

• The skirting above the grey-veined and black marble floor is decorated with Delft tiles. Pottery imitating Chinese porcelain – mainly blue-and-white Ming dynasty ware – from cargoes captured by Dutch merchant ships, began to be manufactured in Delft in the early seventeenth century.

• The young woman's face is built up of touches of colour, sparkling in the highlights. This lack of linear definition is said to reflect Vermeer's use of a camera obscura, an apparatus by which images of distant objects are projected through a convex lens onto a white surface. This resulted in a slightly blurred image with high tonal contrasts.

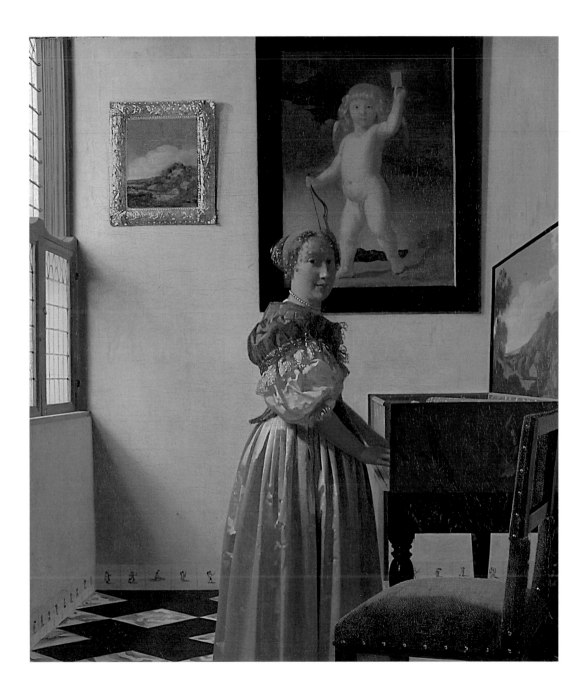

FROM CANALETTO TO CEZANNE
Paintings 1700–1900

There are striking continuities between the paintings here and those in the North Wing: the large, dramatically lit scene staged around a table in Wright of Derby's *An Experiment on a Bird in the Air Pump* is reminiscent of Caravaggio or Rembrandt; earlier portraits are echoed in Ingres's *Madame Moitessier*, while Constable's *The Cornfield* and Turner's *'Fighting Temeraire'* recall the landscapes and harbour scenes of Claude.

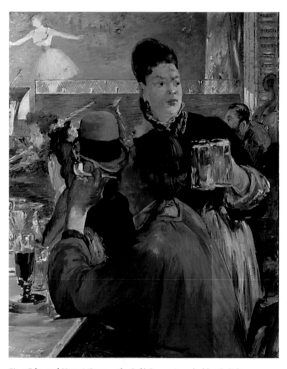

Fig.1 **Edouard Manet** *Corner of a Café-Concert*, probably 1878–80

Yet even in the earliest of these works something new is afoot. Wright of Derby is not illustrating an episode from the Bible, but an anecdote of modern life: not an act of God but a scientific demonstration. Turner celebrates a heroic fighting ship, not a heroic saint, and records the ascendancy of modern steam power; Constable's cornfield ripens under an English sky, with not a glimpse of Roman ruins. If *Madame Moitessier* still evokes an ancient goddess, she does so in the latest fashions of Second Empire Paris. Stubbs's *Whistlejacket* glorifies neither a victorious king nor general, but a winning racehorse. A traditional pictorial

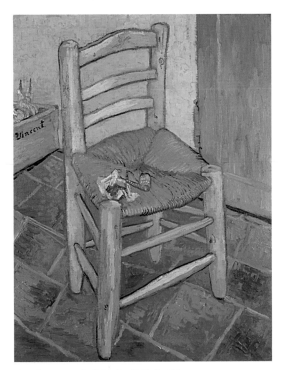

Fig.2 **Vincent van Gogh** *Van Gogh's Chair*, 1888

language speaks of contemporary things – and soon, that language itself will change. In the late nineteenth-century rooms, it is that change which is most readily apparent, in the brilliant colours, the broad-brush shorthand and the seeming spontaneity of Impressionist pictures (fig.1). Monet's *Bathers at La Grenouillère*, conceived as a sketch, is transmuted into a finished painting: an art seemingly as fleeting as the scene it records (viewers may be surprised to hear that the painting is nearly 150 years old). New developments in science and technology inspired Wright of Derby and Turner, but such developments were directly responsible for the way Impressionists painted. Theirs are pictures made to new optical principles, with the aid of newly synthesised pigments and newly invented flat-ferruled brushes; the paints taken outdoors in newly developed collapsible metal tubes. The new merchants of artists' supplies made it possible for painters to retire to the country, to work alone without the support of assistants and apprentices. Art dealers sold their work. Contemporary developments in the patterns of trade also affected art: even those painters most deeply steeped in the European tradition looked beyond, to the newly imported Japanese prints, whose images of the 'floating world' of theatres, tea houses and brothels suggested both the

subject matter and composition of Degas's *Miss La La at the Cirque Fernando*, and whose style influenced Van Gogh (fig.2). And yet it is neither continuity nor novelty that is most forcefully demonstrated in the paintings here. As we observe Seurat's debt, in his *Bathers at Asnières*, to Piero della Francesca, and think back to all the masterpieces of European painting in the other wings of the Gallery, it is the infinite capacity of art for transformation and renewal that moves and excites us.

27. **Whistlejacket** (about 1762)

Oil on canvas   292 × 246.4 cm

This nearly life-size portrait of a rearing horse is generally acknowledged to be Stubbs's masterpiece. It was painted for the Marquess of Rockingham, an owner and connoisseur of race horses – an interest explaining his enthusiasm for Stubbs (from whom Rockingham commissioned several equestrian paintings), student of equine anatomy and specialist of 'sporting pictures'.

Whistlejacket was foaled in 1749, inheriting Arabian blood from both his sire and his dam. He was acquired by Rockingham in the late 1750s, and was put out to stud after winning a gruelling four-mile 2,000 guinea race in 1759. It was at this time that Stubbs painted him twice – the second time with his groom and two other stallions. The contrast between the highly finished, fully three-dimensional horse and the unusual, featureless neutral background gave rise to the story, recorded ten years after the picture was painted, that Rockingham had intended it for an equestrian portrait of King George III, abandoned when he was dismissed as Prime Minister in 1766. Neither the relevant dates nor the painting itself support this hypothesis, probably founded on the tradition of royal equestrian portraits demonstrating the *levade*, the proudest 'air' of *haute école* dressage, which Whistlejacket's natural movement closely resembles.

STUBBS IN
THE NATIONAL GALLERY
Stubbs is represented in the National Gallery by two other, much smaller, pictures combining human and horse portraits and landscape – which he normally painted after and around the figures: *The Milbanke and Melbourne Families*, about 1769, and *A Gentleman driving a Lady in a Phaeton*, 1787.

• Whistlejacket's rear hooves cast a shadow, the only area of the background where space is suggested – a horizontal surface supporting the horse's weight. The shadows, besides focusing attention on the horse's strong legs and fine hooves – typical attributes of the Arabian breed – also show the direction of the light.

• Whistlejacket's head demonstrates other features of the Arabian horse: it is small, with protruding eyes and wide nostrils. Arabians were prized for their stamina, intelligence and character. Under the reign of James I and Charles I, forty-three mares were imported into England and a record, the *General Stud Book*, was begun in which their descendants are inscribed.

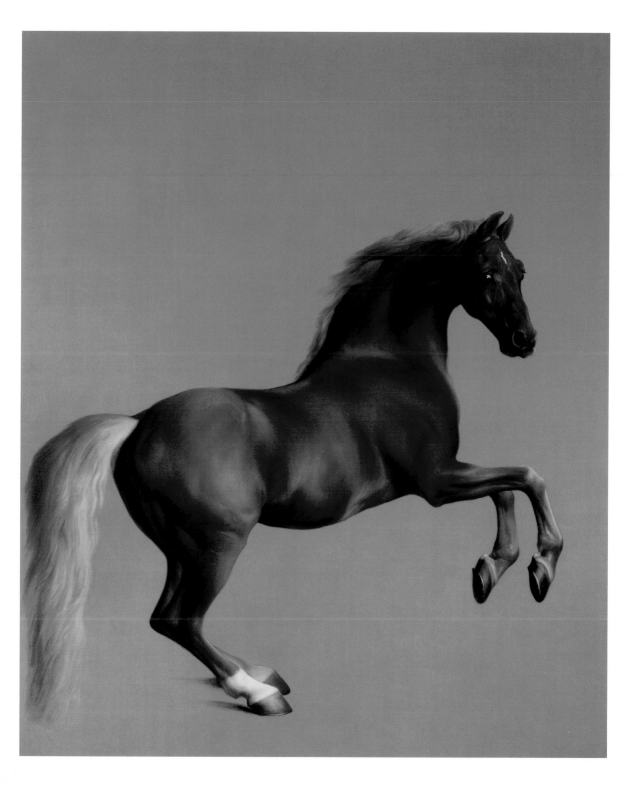

28. An Experiment on a Bird in the Air Pump (1768)

Oil on canvas   182.9 × 243.9 cm

Born in Derby, near England's first large factory, Wright became the poet-painter of the Industrial Revolution. Inspired by the 'candle-light masters' – Dutch followers of Caravaggio – some of whom had worked in England, he interpreted industrial, or, as here, scientific subjects as dramatically lit night scenes. A charismatic 'natural philosopher', the very image of God the Father in traditional religious art, demonstrates the effects of a vacuum. The air has been pumped out of a flask with an air pump; a white cockatoo inside struggles for breath. Its life or death are in the hands of the God-like scientist. A boy, confident the valuable pet will be saved, lowers its cage by the window. A couple on the left have eyes only for each other. All the other participants react to the bird's death throes. The painting's theme of mortality is further elaborated by the traditional motif of a human skull, preserved in the large glass on the table and silhouetted against the light of a single candle.

• The two lovers on the left are Mary Barlow and Thomas Coltman, who were to be married the following year. Their double portrait, *Mr and Mrs Thomas Coltman*, about 1770–2, is Wright's only other painting in the National Gallery. Mary Coltman died in 1786, and Thomas Coltman, who lived until 1826, married again.

• The cockatoo will be saved when the valve at the top of the flask is released, allowing air to enter. The air pump was invented by Otto von Guericke in about 1650. Another of his inventions, the Magdeburg spheres, lies nearby; placed together, and the air pumped out from between them to create a vacuum, the spheres become inseparable.

• Joseph Wright supposedly saw Vesuvius in action during a visit to Italy in 1773–5, after which he added volcanic eruptions to his repertory of night scenes of blacksmiths' shops, iron forges, glass-blowing houses, blast furnaces and cotton mills. He also painted many portraits of friends, mainly manufacturers and engineers.

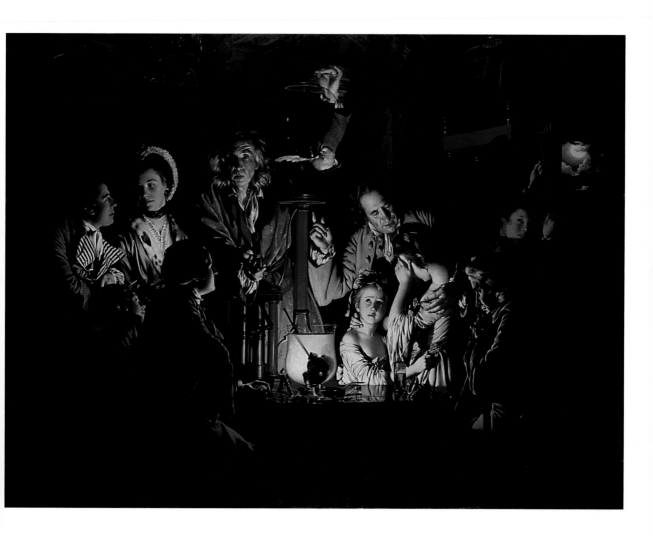

29. **The Cornfield** (1826)

Oil on canvas 142.9 × 121.9 cm

The view is of Fen Lane, which led from Constable's birthplace, East Bergholt, to the village of Dedham. A shepherd boy drinks from the stream, the sheepdog is distracted by a bird, while the sheep head towards an open gate leading to the cornfield where men are harvesting. When the picture was exhibited in 1827, Constable titled it *Landscape, Noon*, attaching lines from Thomson's then famous poem, *Summer*: 'while now a fresher gale, sweeping with shadowy gusts the fields of corn'. This was the first painting by Constable to enter a British public collection; it was purchased by public subscription from his estate after his death in 1837, for presentation to the National Gallery. It remains for many people the artist's most familiar and best-loved work, the very essence of the English countryside on an English summer's day – although, like all the pictures Constable exhibited, it was painted from separate sketches in his studio in London. The vertical format, unusual in a landscape, emphasises the majestic height of the trees; the composition is closely modelled on *Landscape with Hagar and the Angel*, 1646, a work by Claude now in the National Gallery, that inspired Constable to become a landscape painter.

CONSTABLE IN
THE NATIONAL GALLERY
Constable's paintings are mainly to be found at Tate Britain and the Victoria and Albert Museum. Among the six works housed at the National Gallery are the famous *Hay Wain*, 1821, and the oil sketch of *Weymouth Bay: Bowleaze Cove and Jordon Hill*, which was probably painted during Constable's honeymoon in 1816.

• The boy drinking from the stream is a Wordsworthian emblem of care-free childhood close to nature. But he also justifies a patch of bright red near the foreground that Constable painted in imitation of Rubens, whose *Autumn Landscape with a View of Het Steen in the Early Morning*, probably 1636, like Claude's '*Hagar*', also belonged to Constable's patron Sir George Beaumont and influenced the artist.

• Although Constable's paintings, like Claude's landscapes, were generally ideal constructs rather than accurate records of particular places, the village in the background beyond the cornfield is probably intended to represent Dedham.

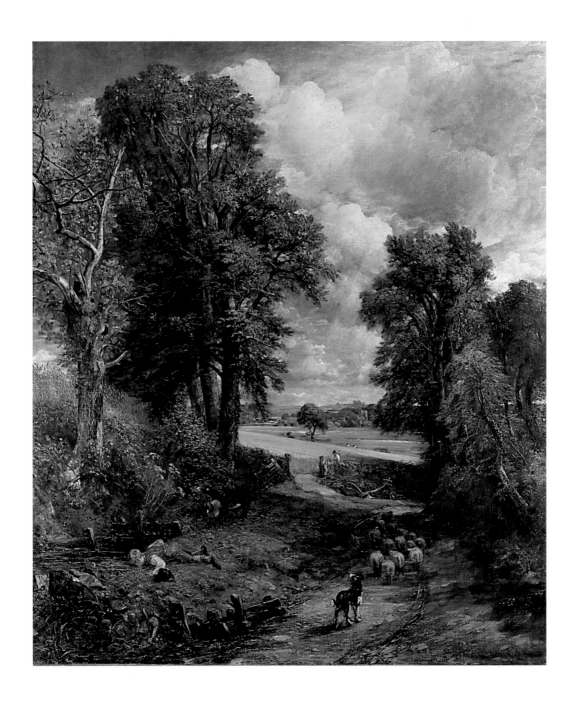

30. The Fighting Temeraire tugged to her Last Berth to be broken up, 1838 (1839)

Oil on canvas 90.8 × 121.9 cm

Turner exhibited this picture in 1839 with the lines, 'The flag which braved the battle and the breeze, No longer owns her'. A warship that had bravely helped to secure victory over the French at Trafalgar in 1805, the *Temeraire* ended her days in the age of steam, sold for the value of her timber to a London ship-breaker. He arranged for her to be towed upstream to his wharf at Rotherhithe. Legend recounts that Turner witnessed her last voyage, but all the evidence is that he painted the picture entirely from imagination – as an essay in patriotism, in homage to the passing of a heroic age, as a meditation on transience and a modern challenge to the majestic luminous harbour scenes of Claude. The ghostly *Temeraire* glides solemnly to its death, towed by a funereal tug belching fire and soot, as the sun sets in glory and a pale new moon rises.

• Searching for the brightest possible sunset hues, Turner painted the sun with a new pigment, barium chromate or 'lemon yellow', which has remained unaltered over time – although fugitive mercuric iodide or 'iodine scarlet', then newly synthesised by Humphry Davy, has caused some fading of the salmon-pink clouds adjoining the darker red sky.

• The *Temeraire*'s masts had, in fact, been removed before it was towed upstream. This is just one example of Turner's use of poetic licence: the hulk was towed by two tugs, solely during daylight hours, over two days following a full moon. To picture a longer plume of smoke, Turner also displaced the tug's funnel.

• '*The Fighting Temeraire*', a painting Turner himself called 'my Darling', inspired several poems and ballads, including a long valedictory by the American novelist and poet Herman Melville, who visited London in 1857, a few months after works bequeathed by Turner to the nation were exhibited in Marlborough House.

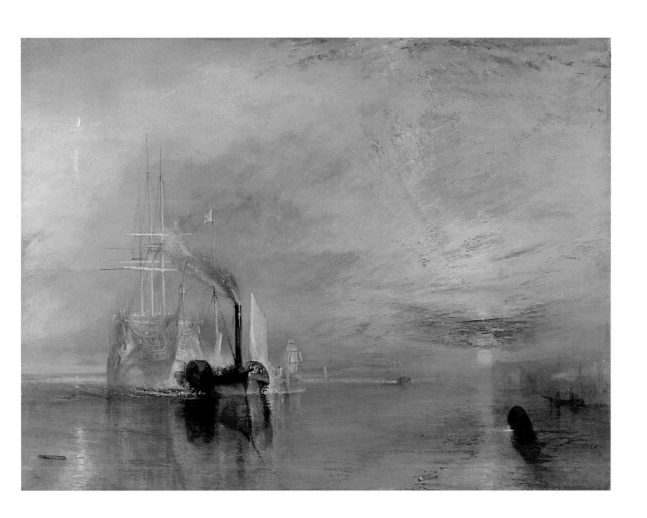

31. **Madame Moitessier** (1856)

Oil on canvas   120 × 92.1 cm

This sumptuous likeness of a wealthy banker's beautiful wife was begun when Inès Moitessier was 26, and finished only when she had turned 35 – and Ingres himself 76. During this time, the artist despaired of completing it several times; in 1853, he described it in a letter to the sitter as 'your portrait, which for too long a time has tormented both of us'. The painting, which now appears so perfectly calculated and in such immaculate condition, is the result of many radical changes made to Mme Moitessier's appearance, to her dress and jewellery and the furnishings of her salon. Ingres originally asked the model to pose with her little daughter, 'la charmante Catherine', but soon banished the child – who was doubtless bored with the long hours of immobility required by the painter. In 1851, having abandoned the sittings, he began anew, after completing a standing likeness of Mme Moitessier dressed in black, now in Washington. Here, surrounded by Second Empire opulence, she sits with her head resting against her forefinger in a pose derived from an ancient Roman wall painting of Arcadia. Transcending the vagaries of high bourgeois fashion, Ingres has made her as ageless, inscrutable and fascinating as the sphinx.

INGRES IN
THE NATIONAL GALLERY
Ingres despised portraiture as a lower form of art, wishing to dedicate himself to 'history painting' and allegory. He became none-the-less one of the greatest portraitists of all time; the National Gallery also owns his *Monsieur de Norvins*, 1811–2, Chief of Police of French-occupied Rome.

• The dress was altered from a plain yellow fabric to this riotously flowered silk from Lyons – woven with bright new aniline dyes – conforming to a shift in fashion during the mid-1850s led by the Empress Eugenie, whose husband, Napoleon III, wished to stimulate the national silk-weaving industry.

• The reflection in the mirror now appears optically impossible, because Ingres altered the painting's original tufted chair into a canapé set parallel to the mirror. Rather than show the back of the sitter's head, however, he must have wished to include her profile, stressing her resemblance to the ancient goddess of the wall painting that inspired her pose.

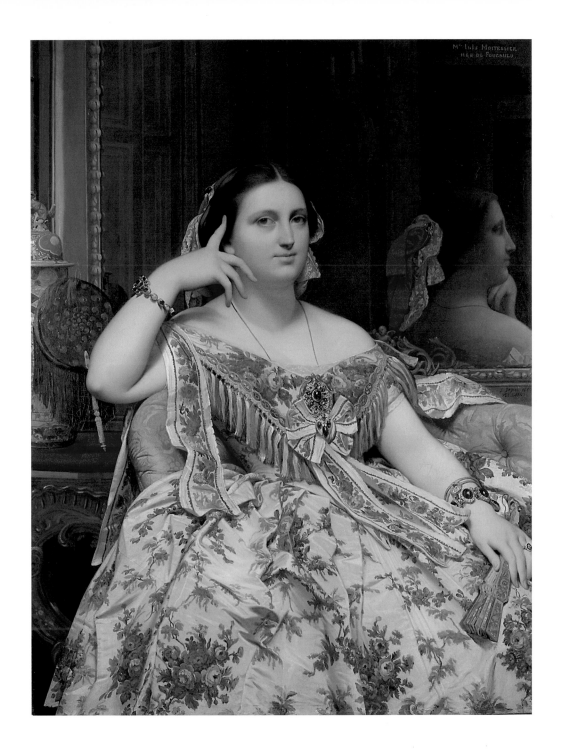

32. **Bathers at La Grenouillère** (1869)

Oil on canvas 73 × 92 cm

Originally intended as no more than a *pochade*, a preliminary study for a large composition to be elaborated from sketches in the studio, this small canvas was later exhibited as complete in itself, becoming one of Monet's most famous 'Impressionist' pictures. It shows La Grenouillère, a raffish resort on the Seine near Paris, where Monet worked side by side with Renoir in the summer of 1869; here with day trippers, bathing cabins, boats for rent and a narrow wooden walkway leading to a round islet called the 'camembert' after the cheese of the same shape. Open-air painting was made easier by the invention of the collapsible metal paint tube and the flat-ferruled paintbrush. Collapsible tubes enabled oil paints – now no longer laboriously hand-ground in the studio but sold by specialist manufacturers – to be stored, soft and ready for use at any time. The new brushes permitted artists to paint coloured patches, or *taches*, rapidly in broad, flat, evenly loaded strokes. Yet even this instantaneous-seeming image, which helped to abolish the traditional distinction between sketch and finished painting, was achieved only after revisions visible even to the naked eye, notably to the position of the boats in the foreground.

• Railways had made the countryside accessible to most Parisians; new cafés and bathing places on the Seine attracted people of all classes. Monet's summary *taches* rapidly define the forms of two women, in daring bathing costumes and 'common' poses, flirting with a figure in the dark coat and light trousers of a bourgeois man-about-town.

• The illusion of reflections in restlessly moving water is created by broken horizontal slabs of colour, painted with the same flat brushes as the figures. Capturing the fleeting effects of natural light was one of the prime objectives of Impressionism. Monet used new synthetic blue pigments that replaced the costly imported lapis lazuli used by painters in previous centuries.

• With his friends Pissarro, Renoir, Degas and others, Monet was one of the founder members of an artists' co-operative that held its first group exhibition in 1874, in defiance of the official Paris Salon. The group were derisively named Impressionists after his sketch-like *Impression, Sunrise*, now in Paris.

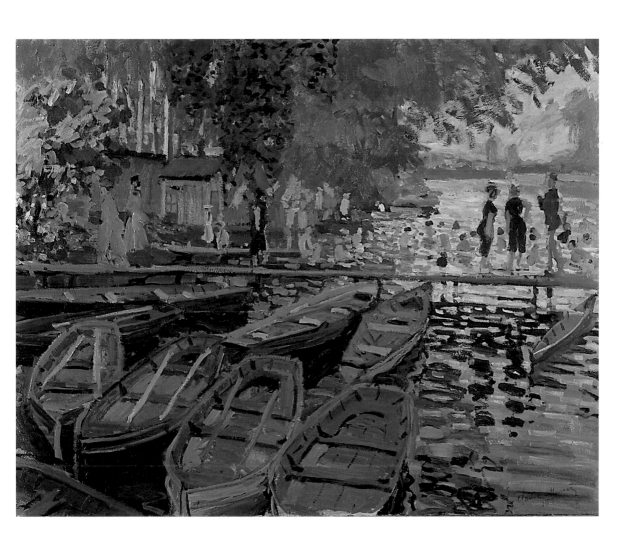

33. **Miss La La at the Cirque Fernando** (1879)

Oil on canvas   116.8 × 77.5 cm

From the late 1860s, Degas specialised in scenes of contemporary life: the ballet, café-concerts, race courses, women at work or at their *toilette*. As the daringly asymmetrical composition of this canvas demonstrates, he was also influenced by the newly imported Japanese prints of modern subjects. Although he participated in all but one of the Impressionist group shows, Degas never entirely shared their ideals: as this painting shows he sought to combine colour with firm drawing; made carefully composed paintings, and explored the effects of artificial lighting. In later life, with failing eyesight, he worked mainly indoors and with pastels.

Miss La La caused a sensation at the Cirque Fernando in Paris, performing various feats of strength. Degas, relying on many sketches made of her act on the spot, shows her being pulled up to the full height of the circus dome as she would have appeared to a member of the audience craning upwards to see her from below. The direction of the light, placed to coincide with our view point, accentuates the fore-shortening of her face and the diagonals of her arms and legs, parallel to the receding lines of the rafters.

DEGAS IN
THE NATIONAL GALLERY

Degas, deeply devoted to academic tradition and a pupil of pupils of Ingres, began as a painter of narrative subjects drawn from history. One of his most important works in this genre, *Young Spartans Exercising*, about 1860, based on a text by the ancient Greek writer Plutarch, is in the National Gallery.

• Miss La La was an acrobat of mixed race. Her most spectacular feat, as shown by Degas, was to be lifted up by a cable clenched between her teeth. The Cirque Fernando was located on the corner of the boulevard Rochechouart and the rue des Martyrs.

• The perspective construction of this picture is especially complex, and may reflect Degas's observation of Italian art during his study tour in 1856–9. The figure is shown in the 'oblique perspective' of Veronese's ceiling paintings: from below and to the side. The building, presumably twelve-sided, seems to extend beyond the canvas and thus behind the spectator.

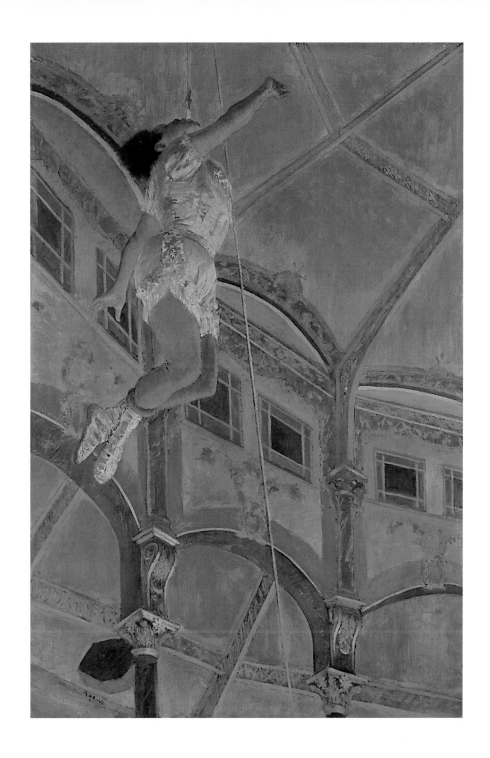

34. **Self Portrait** (about 1880–1)

Oil on canvas 33.6 × 26 cm

Cézanne, the great interpreter of landscape and still life, continued to experiment with portraiture throughout his career. This small, unostentatious bust-length self portrait shows him at about forty-one years of age, when he was still financially dependent on his tyrannical father – a rich banker who wanted him to become a lawyer – and increasingly isolated from his friends. Severely objective, the painting gives no hint either of the sitter's personality or of his profession. Under Pissarro's guidance, Cézanne had learnt the techniques and theories of the Impressionists; now, although he still used the broken patches of colour that were their trademark, he chose to emphasise three-dimensional form and two-dimensional pattern rather than describe the fleeting effects of natural light. In this picture, form and pattern are integrated across the whole canvas. The raised notched collar of Cézanne's coat, on the right, echoes the diamond pattern of the wallpaper, setting up a diagonal that runs through the sitter's mouth, beard and ear – a dynamic line that founders in the strict vertical of the blue area on the left. And while the domed skull remains forcefully three-dimensional, the shaded side of the face has been flattened and brought forward to the picture surface.

CEZANNE IN
THE NATIONAL GALLERY
Among Cézanne's works in the National Gallery are an early portrait of his father painted directly on the plaster wall of the salon in the family home near Aix-en-Provence in about 1862, and one of the three great canvases of his old age, *Bathers* (*Les Grandes Baigneuses*), about 1900–6.

• Seen in isolation, Cézanne's eyes appear almost as if he were painted in full-face – only the direction of the glance indicates that his head is turned away in three-quarter profile, causing him to look sideways at the viewer. The eye on our right is darker, since it is in shadow.

• The diamond-patterned wallpaper, that itself combines dynamic diagonals with static horizontals and verticals, was painted several times by Cézanne. Here, it helps him to realise the aim of his mature style (that later influenced the Cubists Braque, Picasso and Gris): to represent three-dimensional structure simultaneously with flat design, integrating the foreground figure with its background.

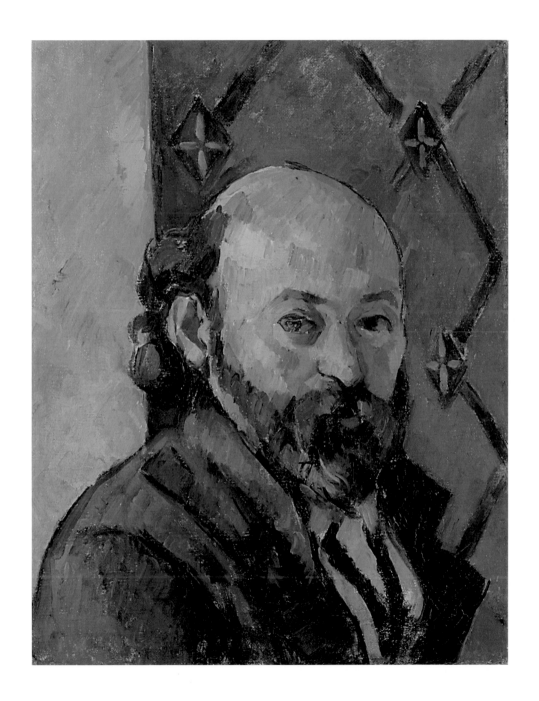

35. **Bathers at Asnières** (1884)

Oil on canvas 201 × 300 cm

The setting for this, the first of Seurat's large-scale paintings, is a stretch of the River Seine in north-west Paris between the bridges at Asnières and Courbevoie. In the distance are the large factories at Clichy; in the foreground industrial workers relax on their day of rest. Seurat's theme of proletarian recreation was topical, a concern of radical politicians and of the Realist writers of the day. Ostensibly, his treatment carries no overt social comment, but its large scale and geometric grandeur relate it to the heroic 'history paintings' of an earlier age – most particularly to the frescoes painted by Piero della Francesca for Arezzo, which Seurat would have studied in replica in the chapel of the Ecole des Beaux-Arts in Paris. The original handling of the paint – which predates the development of Seurat's famed pointillist technique – varied from thick Impressionist brush-strokes in the river to a criss-cross of pink, orange, yellow and green lines in the grass. As in his masterly black-and-white conté crayon drawings, the figures are irradiated by manipulating the background tones with no regard to optical reality: the water turns dark behind highlighted flesh, and appears bright behind flesh in shadow.

SEURAT IN
THE NATIONAL GALLERY
Preparatory oil sketches for this picture and for Seurat's next great work, *Sunday Afternoon on the Island of La Grande Jatte*, now in Chicago, were presented to the National Gallery in 1995 when one of Seurat's last paintings, *The Channel of Gravelines*, 1890, fully pointillist in technique, was also acquired.

• The red hat was reworked by Seurat using the pointillist technique he adapted from Impressionist colour theory: the hat was modelled by adding spots of pure blue and yellow, intense, contrasting colours that are meant to produce an optical mixture on the viewer's retina without muddying the colours as do paints mixed on the palette.

• The couple with parasol and top hat being ferried across the river under the blue, white and red flag of the Third Republic, are bourgeois – on their way to the middle-class resort of La Grande Jatte, the setting of Seurat's next monumental work.

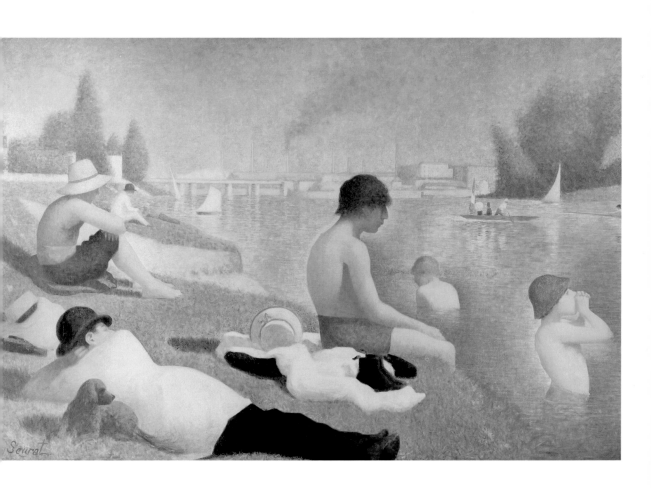

36. **Sunflowers** (1888)

Oil on canvas 92 × 73 cm

In February 1888, Vincent van Gogh, dreaming of founding an artists' colony 'close to nature' in the south of France, left Paris for Arles. The painter Paul Gauguin agreed to join him, and in the summer, before Gauguin's arrival in October, Van Gogh began a dazzling series of pictures of sunflowers to welcome 'the new poet [who will be] living here'. He painted four canvases before the flowers faded, but considered only two – of which this is one – good enough to sign and hang in Gauguin's bedroom (the other is now in Munich). 'To get up enough heat to melt those golds . . . it's not everyone that can do it, it takes the energy and concentration of a person's whole being…', Van Gogh wrote to his brother Theo. In January of 1889 he also painted three 'absolutely equal and identical copies'.

The London *Sunflowers* is Van Gogh's first successful experiment in painting 'light on light'. Its predominant yellow colour – at once decorative and, for the painter, an emblem of happiness – is also a tribute to a contemporary artist, Adolphe Monticelli, who 'depicted the south all in yellow, all in orange, all in sulphur'. The flowers illustrate the cycle of life from bud through maturity and death; their spiky natural forms also evoke human passions. But it would be wrong to see evidence here, as some have done, of artistic 'frenzy'. It is Van Gogh's control of his materials and masterly technique that make this luminous still life so lifelike and so expressive.

VAN GOGH IN
THE NATIONAL GALLERY

Van Gogh's *Chair* shows the artist's 'wooden rush-bottomed chair' in daylight. This picture contrasts with a painting – entitled *Gauguin's Chair* (Rijksmuseum, Amsterdam) – of 'an armchair, red and green . . . on the seat two novels and a candle'. The two paintings contrast Gauguin's belief in an art nourished by literature with Van Gogh's own approach to art based on a feeling for nature.

• Van Gogh exploited the stiff consistency of the newly developed, ready-made machine-ground paints to reproduce on canvas the rough texture of the sunflowers' bristling seedheads and hairy green sepals. The flow of vigorous longer brush-strokes matches the twists and turns of petals, leaves and stems

• Unlike the gnarled and lifelike natural forms of the sunflowers, the thinly-painted table top and vase are simplified, flattened and outlined, recalling Japanese woodcuts or crude popular prints. Van Gogh's signature, 'Vincent', becomes a naïve blue decoration in the glaze of the Provençal earthenware jar.

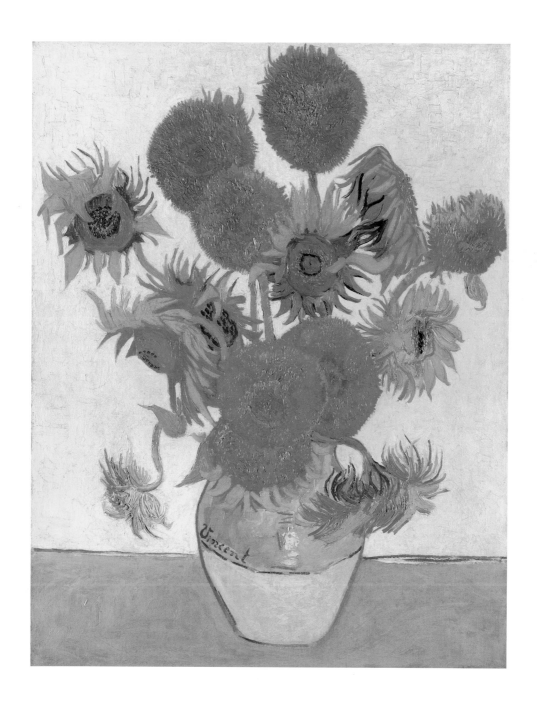

First published in Great Britain in 2000 by
National Gallery Company Limited
St Vincent House
30 Orange Street
London WC2H 7HH

www.nationalgallery.co.uk
Supporting the National Gallery

ISBN-10: 1 85709 373 9
ISBN-13: 978 1 85709 373 5
525371

British Library Cataloguing-in-Publication Data
A catalogue record is available from the British Library

Front cover: detail of Van Gogh, *Sunflowers*, 1888 (36)
Page 2: detail of Claude, *Seaport with the Embarkation of
Saint Ursula*, 1641 (23)
Page 4: detail of Michelangelo, *The Entombment*, about 1500–1 (9)
Page 6: detail of Ingres, *Madame Moitessier*, 1856 (31)

Design Philip Lewis
Editor Tom Windross

Printed and bound in Hong Kong by
Printing Express